I have had the joy of knowing and ministering with Elizabeth Woodson for the better part of a decade. She lives what she writes in these pages. Each of us must come to terms with the distance between the life we pictured and the life we have. The wise Christ-follower navigates that gap with trustworthy disciplines that turn our hearts heavenward. Elizabeth offers up these tools not just as a faithful Bible teacher but as a faithful practitioner. Is longing your companion? Look here for help.

Jen Wilkin, author and Bible teacher

In her book *Embrace Your Life*, Elizabeth is honest and transparent, writing as a friend, as she shares her own journey with longing and the biblical truth that helped her be an overcomer. Elizabeth's words are deeply rooted in Scripture and overflowing with practical wisdom. This book is a true gift and will encourage anyone of any age who is navigating a season of longing and disappointment.

Dr. Tony Evans, president, The Urban Alternative and senior pastor, Oak Cliff Bible Fellowship

How are we to navigate the inevitable disappointments of life in a fallen world? Those seasons when we become painfully aware that life hasn't gone the way we thought it would? I have found over the years that the best guides are the ones who have been there already—the ones who have become acquainted with heartbreak and frustration but have not given in to bitterness. The ones who know anger and despair but are still marked by the peace that passes understanding and the unwavering joy of knowing they belong to Jesus. Elizabeth Woodson is such a guide. She is steeped in the Scriptures but doesn't give in to the vague spiritual sentimentalism that is often dishonest about how much disappointment hurts. She's here to lift our heads, and she has had her head lifted by others. She is with us in this valley of longing, and writes with empathy and compassion while not being afraid to say what is true.

Matt Chandler, lead pastor, The Village Church

ELIZABETH WOODSON

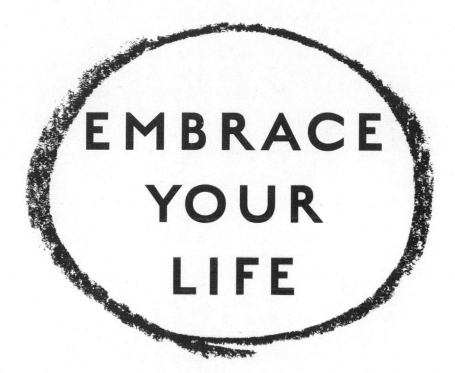

EMBRACE YOUR LIFE

HOW TO FIND JOY WHEN THE LIFE YOU
HAVE IS NOT THE LIFE YOU HOPED FOR

B&H
PUBLISHING
NASHVILLE, TENNESSEE

For Evelyn McNeil Woodson, M.Ed.
*Nana, you never gave up and never
stopped chasing your dreams.*

For Nono
You never stop fighting to live.

Acknowledgments

Thank you, Mom and Dad, for loving me, supporting me, and showing me that my best life is in Jesus.

Thank you, Jan, for believing in me.

Thank you, Erik, Ashley, and the B&H team, for making my words beautiful.

Thank you to the family and friends who prayed for me, listened to my ideas, and celebrated the writing of this book with me.

Contents

Introduction

Embrace the Journey

During my first few years in Dallas, there was a woman—we'll call her Charlene—who was a part of my small group.[1] Like other small groups you may have been a part of, we started off by sharing our life stories. When it was her turn, Charlene talked about how she was enduring a hard season in her marriage—an overwhelming situation that was now spilling over into difficulty with her adult children. Hers was a story that included divorce, abuse, and now an estranged relationship with a son who had just had a baby with his girlfriend. Charlene was overwhelmed and hurt because he wouldn't let her see the baby. This particular evening she'd had enough, and as she was talking about the latest experience of struggle she screamed out, *"This is not how my life was supposed to turn out. It wasn't supposed to be this way!"*

After the meeting ended, all I could think of was what Charlene had said. Her words were so honest and pregnant with pain. Unfortunately, my own story was full of this kind of painful disappointment. Whether it was a hard job experience or a romantic relationship that had soured, I knew what it was like to long for a life I didn't have. I knew what it was like to feel helpless, looking around at your life wondering, *How did I get here?* or thinking, *I never thought life would turn out like **this***.

And you know what? I don't think this feeling of disappointment is unique to either me or Charlene. I think many people deal with it, including you. It's probably one of the reasons you chose to pick up this book.

The prolonged disappointment that you and I—and many others—experience is what I like to call "longing"—the emotional response to the gap between the life you hoped for and the one you actually have. You and I have a set of expectations about how our lives should turn out. You may have expected marriage to be easy, expected to be able to conceive a child, or expected your hard work to turn into financial success. But when marriage is difficult (or nonexistent), infertility persists, or your business collapses, hope can feel so far away. In these moments, it seems as if life has disappointed you and left you with more questions than answers.

Like many experiences in life, longing presents all sorts of questions. But one particular problem with longing is that those questions tend not to have easy answers. And the hardest part is that we don't discover this until we exhaust ourselves by throwing quick fixes at our problems. Have you ever done this? It's the moment we've done so many Google searches to find an answer and finally reached that last page of results— that one that exists in some dark corner of the internet—only to realize there's no real solution there. We've asked all our friends, pastors, or coworkers for help, only to receive pity or shallow band-aid statements to cover the wound. Lastly, we've asked God for help, a lot. But when prayer after prayer is not answered the way we want, we can become disillusioned, not knowing how to move forward or rebuild the dreams that have crumbled. This disillusionment can persist for a long time, causing our souls to become emotionally weary as we tire from the burden of carrying the weight of our despair.

Like I said, I know what it feels like because I've been there.

Currently, I'm a never-married single in my late thirties. Now, before you put this book down, know this is not a book about singleness. But over the years my singleness has taught me so much about the longing I believe *we all* experience. So before I dig into your stories, I thought it best to share my own.

I'm not particularly sure when it got there, but marriage has always held a spot on my "life goals" list. I didn't think about when it would happen, but I always assumed at some point it would.

I graduated from high school with no high school sweetheart to potentially marry. I then went to college and graduated, still unmarried. I started working and got another degree, and was still as single as a dollar bill. Finally, I left my job, went to seminary, and then eventually got hired at a church where I led a ministry that was supposed to help single people get married. And the fruit of all that? You guessed it: I didn't get married.

I had accomplished most of the major goals, except the one that hovered at the top of my list. So, around my late twenties-early-thirties I started to entertain the question that most singles love to avoid: "What if I never get married?" The consideration of this question was not me giving up on the possibility of marriage, but rather me figuring out what to do with my sadness. No one seemed to have good answers for me—most of them made marriage merit-based or told me I didn't have enough faith. I knew enough about God to know that neither of those answers were true, but I still didn't know how to live in the gap between the life I had hoped for and the life I had.

Shallow answers tend to frustrate me, so for the next few years I wrestled with God and my Bible to find substantive ones. I wanted an answer that would be true, regardless of whether it ended up being the answer I preferred. Moreover, I wanted an answer that had the power to not simply pacify me, but to release me to experience a full and vibrant life. I wanted to know how to have a life that, despite my longing, provided me with true and lasting joy.

A Journey to Find Joy

I'll be honest, I'm not a fan of affirmation circles. Have you heard of them? They are where there's a chair in the middle of a circle, and everyone in the circle takes turns sitting in the chair while they receive affirming messages from the group. The reason I don't like them isn't because I don't like encouraging other people; it's because sitting in a circle with everyone looking at you makes me extremely uncomfortable.

A few years ago, I found myself in an affirmation circle that initially proved to be just as uncomfortable as every other one I had been a part of. I sat in a chair while awkwardly waiting for people to give me encouraging words. But, after a bit of silence, one of the group members offered me an unexpected yet very encouraging compliment. She said, "Elizabeth, you do what lots of folks think is impossible. You live your single life with so much joy." In her short statement, I felt like her words highlighted a turning point in my life, because she was right. I did have joy, lots of it.

At that moment I realized that I had found what I had been searching for. The road had not been easy, but after years of wrestling with the Lord, he had not necessarily changed my situation, but he had changed *me*. He had graciously allowed me to embody the joy I had been hoping to find.

Now, even though the process didn't take me in a straight line, there were some distinct places the Lord took me. In fact, I like to think of them as spiritual exercises or practices that he took me through. During my journey the practices of *self-examination, lament, hope, remembrance, faith,* and *joy* gave me the renewed perspective I needed to embrace the life God had given me.

The goal of our time together is to take you on this same journey, making those same six stops along the way. We'll begin by talking through the heart of each spiritual practice and then, at the end of each chapter, I'll help you apply what you learned. Theology is needed and beautiful, but it isn't just meant to take up space in our head. What we believe should affect the way we live. So, as I invite you into a space of discovery, I will help you make sure that your insights don't remain theoretical, but run down deep into the entirety of your life.

And, even though I've learned a lot from my time with the Lord, the specific story we'll follow won't be mine. We'll use one you are probably familiar with—the Bible's story. Why? Because the key to our joy is connected to us understanding that we are a part of a story that is bigger than our pain. So, it is the story of the Bible that will give us perspective and revive our joy. But we won't cover the entire Bible; we'll just focus on one short story.

Our Guide for the Journey

Navigating our longing can be a confusing and complicated process. But having a friend to walk you through the season can be helpful, especially when that friend has experienced longing themselves. The more I've grown in my walk with the Lord, the more I've come to realize that he has provided us with some great "friends" in Scripture. In the Bible, there is wisdom and solace in the lives of other people of faith who have walked this earth thousands of years before you and me.

One such friend is Joshua.

When we meet him, Joshua is experiencing a major turning point in his life. He is thrown into a major leadership role, one that gives him influence over a few million people. While many of us might think that sounds exciting, we also find that at this same time, Joshua is also walking in a place of longing.

In fact, the longing will not leave him before he steps into his new role; but rather, it goes with him.

As we consider this season of transition in Joshua's life, we will zoom in on a brief conversation he has with God. Even though it is only a few verses, what God says to Joshua will be full of rich theological truth for us. These verses will also serve as a guide to help us understand how to navigate our own season of longing, because in a short period of time we will see God invite Joshua into a place of *self-examination, lament, hope, remembrance, faith,* and *joy.* In fact, as we fast-forward to the end of Joshua's life, we will see that the seeds planted by this conversation end up bearing fruit in his life until the very end.

Friend, I don't know what longing looks like for you today. I don't know the story behind the disappointment you bear, nor do I know the specifics of your disillusionment or despair. I don't know which life you wish you could wake up to each morning. But I do know what it's like to wrestle with God over the story you wish you had; and I want to tell you this: the joy you seek is possible to find. And, it's not a cheesy joy that minimizes our pain. It's a deep and substantive joy that has enough strength to handle your hard questions, yet is soft enough to handle your tears too. By the time you finish this book, I can't promise you that your situation will change. But my hope is that you will find a renewed vision for your life— one that is worth living because you see the beauty of the One you get to live it with.

Chapter I

Embrace Help

I love watching home renovations on TV. So on the rare occasion I'm actually watching TV, I tend to only watch HGTV or The DIY channel.[1] One of my favorite home renovation shows is *Holmes Inspection*. It's a show about people who have major problems with their homes. Whether it's a huge leak in the basement, a crumbling foundation, or heating/cooling issues, these folks are usually at their wits' end. So, they reach out to the main star of the show, Mike Holmes, to come help them out. Mike is an experienced contractor and home inspector who will come and assess the situation. Then he and his team will fix the issue.

The common thread between all the episodes is that although the homeowner can generally see they have an issue, they tend not to know how deep it goes. During his inspection, Mike will start by examining the clear indicators of damage, like a pool of water on the basement floor. He will then pull up the floor or pull back the walls to find that the real problem is a cracked foundation or a wall that is crumbling because of termites. As an inspector, Mike is able to look beneath the surface to help the homeowners understand the *roots* of their problems.

It can be hard to recognize the roots of our longing because, if we're honest, we're all masters at masking it with certain behaviors or thought patterns. Often this masking is subconscious, as we do our best to navigate life. It is also different for each person, with everyone having a unique set of behaviors or thought patterns they use to immediately soothe any discomfort or pain that might arise in their soul.

For some of us, our value and identity are closely tied to who we are or what we do. For high achievers, when expectations about a particular situation or relationship are not met, we will not only see the *situation* as a failure, but will attach that label to *ourselves*. In response, we might experience an onslaught of negative thoughts and speech toward ourselves or others. These overly critical words become a slow-dripping tool of destruction. In the moment, we don't realize the damage our words are doing to us and others. But the depth of our sadness sometimes produces strong and powerful language that keeps us in a cycle of despair.

Or maybe it's not negative thought patterns for you. Maybe, if you are anything like me in moments of longing, you find it easier to drown out all that negative noise by focusing all of your efforts on seeking comfort. I can find myself believing that, *If I'm comfortable, then everything will be okay.* All that's needed is one more meal, one more drink, one more show to binge, one more hours-long session scrolling through social media, one more text from an ex, one more random trip to Target, or one more [fill in the blank with your favorite comfort-coping mechanism]. I wish I could say I haven't consciously or subconsciously said this to myself, but I have. I've learned the hard way that trying to combat pain by filling up on things that I think will make me feel good doesn't work. As much as you and I might try, nothing can fully ease or soothe our pain but the Lord.

Or maybe you don't drown out the negative stuff. Maybe you turn it all the way up, and instead of directing it inward, you direct it upward. After all, knowing that God has the power to intervene in your life, but sometimes chooses not to do so in the ways you want him to, is a hard truth to accept. So instead of solemn disappointment, some of us process our *real* emotions by becoming angry with God, who we feel is responsible for our pain. We raise our fist and shake it at him with a barrage of "Why?" questions that are almost entirely unanswerable. We wanted easy explanations. We wanted God's ways to match our plans. But they didn't. And now, well, *heaven's gonna hear about it.*

No matter what it looks like for you in your darkest hour, your longing can feel overwhelming and lies can sound like truth. So please know this, friend: you are not a failure, your pain is not the enemy, and God has not abandoned you. He is present with you in your pain and is able to bring you the healing that your soul desires.

But, in order to experience God's healing, you and I first have to recognize the symptoms of our longing. In other words, when there is water dripping from the ceiling of our

lives, we need to pay attention. Self-deprecation, overly negative thoughts and speech, over-consumption of any kind, and/
or anger with God are all signs that we have a deep source of
pain that needs to be addressed. And then, instead of only
focusing on the surface issue, (for example, trying to indulge
in food or entertainment a little less often, or practicing posi-
tive self-talk), we have to go deeper than that. We have to get
honest about the source—the roots—of our longing.

But like the folks on that home renovation show I mentioned previously, we can't go through this examination process alone.

We need help.

Learning from Joshua

Joshua first appears in Exodus 17, where he is chosen by
Moses to lead Israel in a battle against the Amalekites. You may
already be familiar with his story, but to recap it for you, Joshua
was one of the hundreds of thousands of people Moses helped
deliver from Egypt. He was born a slave and, through the grace
of God, found freedom. Early into Israel's story, Joshua is identified as a leader, and after his victory in Exodus 17, he is chosen
to join eleven other men as a spy. Moses tasked these men to
explore the land of Canaan, the land God had promised to give
Israel. When these spies came back from their trip, only two of
them gave a good report. Joshua was one of those men.

During Israel's decades of wandering in the wilderness,
Joshua became Moses's servant and one of his most trusted
and courageous captains. For those forty years, Joshua served

Moses faithfully. And then, right before Israel is finally set to lay claim to the land of Canaan, Moses shares these words with Joshua and the entire nation of Israel:

> "I am 120 years old today. I am no longer able to go out and come in. The LORD has said to me, 'You shall not go over this Jordan.' The LORD your God himself will go over before you. He will destroy these nations before you, so that you shall dispossess them, and Joshua will go over at your head, as the LORD has spoken. And the LORD will do to them as he did to Sihon and Og, the kings of the Amorites, and to their land, when he destroyed them. And the LORD will give them over to you, and you shall do to them according to the whole commandment that I have commanded you. Be strong and courageous. Do not fear or be in dread of them, for it is the LORD your God who goes with you. He will not leave you or forsake you." (Deut. 31:2–6)

At this moment, Moses is announcing his impending death. He would not be leading Israel through this pivotal moment in their history. Joshua would experience the fulfillment of a forty-year journey without the man who had led the nation through it all. But Moses did not leave Joshua empty-handed. In Deuteronomy 34:9, we are told that, "Now Joshua son of Nun was filled with the *spirit of wisdom* because Moses had laid his hands on him. So the Israelites listened to him and did what the LORD had commanded Moses" (NIV, emphasis added).

While we see the Holy Spirit permanently indwell believers in the New Testament, in the Old Testament he temporarily indwells certain people to help them achieve specific tasks.[2] Joshua is one of these people, and by the power and help of the Spirit, he had been given the wisdom he needed to navigate his season of longing. At any particular point in time, this wisdom would allow him to assess his situation and determine whether or not he was on the right track. Said another way, the spirit of wisdom would help Joshua examine himself, so that he could make the adjustments that would enable him, and Israel, to experience the fullness of life that God had set out for them.

Because of Christ, the same spirit of wisdom that was given to Joshua lives in all believers (Eph. 1:17). The Holy Spirit has been given to us that we might have the help we need to live the life we have been given, especially in seasons of longing. The writers of the New Testament tell us that the Holy Spirit will guide us (John 16:13–15), teach us (John 14:26), pray for us (Rom. 8:26), and provide us with wisdom (Acts 6:10; 1 Cor. 2:12–14; 12:8; Col. 1:9). But, like God the Father and God the Son, God the Holy Spirit is also all-knowing. Nothing gets past him. In the same way that he did for Joshua, the Holy Spirit helps us examine our lives and make the adjustments we need to experience the joy that, through Christ, is available to us. So, even though we may be able to see our longing, we need the Holy Spirit, as the divine heart inspector, to pull up the floors of our life to show us what the *root* of our longing actually is.

Friend, if you hear anything at this point, let me encourage you with this: *the Holy Spirit is your Helper. You don't have to go at this alone. He is present with you and wants to help you. Embrace his help.*

The Root of Our Longing

The truth is, God's Spirit should be our primary influence as we navigate our longing. But sometimes we don't give him much room to help us because we're already being "helped" by a whole host of other influences—ones that have created all sorts of expectations about life. These expectations come from lots of different people and places. Many of them were shaped by our family. For better or worse, our childhood home was the place that developed our thoughts of how the world should function. It's where we learned what love looked like and what it meant to be an adult.

I wonder how your upbringing shaped your expectations about life. Maybe you learned that you should be treated with honor and dignity, no matter who you are or where you're from. Perhaps you inherited an assumption that life was supposed to be free from suffering and pain. Or maybe you were raised to desire love, harmony, and oneness. Perhaps none of that is true, and you grew up in a broken home, learning that chaos is the way of the world and only the clever and the tough will make it in the end—that joy is reserved for those brave enough to leave all that craziness behind and go chase down the good life for themselves.

Because of these influences, you likely expected that in some way life would be full of goodness and joy, whether that life would be handed to you or hunted down yourself. You may have also learned to expect that you will always have control over the outcome of your life. Nothing, including finances, health, and relational commitments, should prevent you from having all that you desire. In the words of the good ol' American adage, *if you believe it, then you can achieve it!*

But your family unit isn't the only place your expectations come from. You and I have also been heavily influenced by the media. Here's the truth: you and I probably spend too much time online looking at other people's lives! The digital descriptions and images of the "perfect" lives that we are bombarded with on a daily basis shape our expectation of who we should be and what we should have. We see countless pictures showing other people's joy and want to have the same. We want what we think they have: their happy marriage, beautiful appearance, perfectly behaved children, or successful career. As we virtually consume the lives of others, our hearts begin to crave attention, accolades, and superiority. We want to have the best and be the best, and anything that falls short of this goal becomes an immediate disappointment.

As I've wrestled with my own feelings of longing, I've come to believe that whether they are reasonable or not, prolonged disappointment from unmet expectations is caused by the same root—*idealism*. This is the belief that what I have is not enough and that true joy would be found in something "better." In my mind, the good life happens when everything is as I believe it should be, when real life lines up with my ideal life.

For instance, most of my female friends are single and I can't count the amount of conversations I've had where one of them says, "I never thought I'd be single this long." And, as years turn into decades, these conversations have grown to include a sadness for what they believe they've lost. Some have given up hope for children and others seem stuck in a holding pattern waiting for life to start. Especially for older singles, despair can be a close companion because hope for marriage seems to have evaporated. The life they want seems so far away from the life they have, which makes finding joy in this season an almost impossible task. The good life for them is not in their singleness but is found in what they don't have—marriage.

Similar to my single friends, we all have envisioned what an ideal life would be like. Yet, when we take a hard look at this "ideal life," what we are imagining is usually a life in which we give priority to our own superiority, comfort, and pleasure, allowing these things to be the standard by which we determine what is best. While it's certainly not wrong to desire something good that God has made, we live in a world that tells you and me to prioritize our personal desires to the level of demands, and that the time for their fulfillment is right now. This expectation of immediate gratification inevitably adds to our disappointment, leading us to abandon patience as hope quickly fades.

Pulling Up the Root

Friend, your healing can only come when you are able to process your pain with clarity and conviction. This means that the longing that emerges from unmet expectations is a signal, a symptom, revealing a larger issue that needs to be addressed.

First, with the help of the Holy Spirit, you and I have to acknowledge where our expectations have come from and determine whose glory they are rooted in. Sometimes our expectations about life are reasonable. After all, we all crave the kind of goodness that is linked to the character and nature of God. However, sometimes our expectations, because they are not based in God's truth, are unreasonable. In fact, our misplaced expectations can cause us to elevate our own glory over God's glory.

To live for God's glory means that his purposes take priority over yours and mine. When our way and his way conflict, we choose to follow his way. But when we choose to prioritize the fulfillment of our desires over his, we are living for our own glory. When our expectations about life cause us to demand outcomes that contradict the truth of God's Word, we are claiming that we know better than God does. And, in doing so we make ourselves the god of our own lives. It's at this moment that the Holy Spirit helps us remember that, as A. W. Tozer says, "God knows us better than we know ourselves, and He knows exactly what we need and when we need it."[3] So, when things in life don't go as planned, the Holy Spirit will help us to submit to God's sovereignty.

Now, living for God's glory and trusting in his sovereignty does not invalidate the very real sorrow and pain of life situations—just like my mom always says, life is hard. But in the midst of hardship, disillusionment, and even failure, we must remember that God has been, is, and always will be good, and living for his glory really is better than living for our own. This means that no matter the season, our good God is always providing blessings for his children, and that his plans can always be trusted. Even still, I know that while Scripture reveals these truths over and over again, it can be hard to feel as if they are true. This is why it's so important for you and me to remember that while our feelings are real, they aren't always reliable. In seasons of longing, we have to keep our head and heart aligned, remembering that what we may feel about God does not dictate his character. God is always exercising his perfect plan for your life. There will be moments when you believe and feel this without much work, and other moments when you have to choose to believe this while you wait for your feelings to catch up.

If you want to know what this looks like, consider David's words in the Psalms. One thing I love about David is that he doesn't shy away from the very real pain and longings he feels. He cries out in his anguish, "O Lord, all my *longing* is before you; my sighing is not hidden from you" (Ps. 38:9, emphasis added). David doesn't keep his longings hidden! Whether it is safety, or companionship, or vindication, he doesn't sweep them under the rug. He opens them up before God over and over. He is willing to be honest about them and bring them to the Lord so that he might leave them in better hands than his own. Yet, in many other places, we see that among his many longings, he has one ultimate love: "O Lord, I *love* the habitation of your house and the place where *your glory* dwells. . . . My soul is consumed with *longing* for your rules at all times" (Pss. 26:8; 119:20, emphasis added).[4] David's ultimate longing was for God's glory and God's Word. While other desires surely mattered, these are what won out in his heart. The same could be said of Jesus in the garden of Gethsemane, where he longed for the possibility for the story of redemption to play out some other way, and was honest about that desire, and yet ultimately chose the way of the Father's will (Matt. 26:39). He chose the Father's plan right in the middle of real and raw emotions. In these cases and more, we see that longing for something isn't the problem. In fact, we should bring our longing into the presence of God. Rather, elevating our longing to the point of ultimacy is the problem along with allowing those longings to dictate our view of God.

Second, you and I have to remember (also through the help of the Spirit!) the truth about reality—that as humans living in a sinful world, we will live in a constant state of imperfection until Jesus returns. You don't have to look far to see that things in this world aren't as they should be. Death, sickness, violence, and exploitation are only a few of the many forms of brokenness that exist. No one should be okay with the expectation that their life might be wounded by the sin of another person, but far too often that is our reality.

In the beginning, God created humanity in his image and called us "very good" (Gen. 1:31). Our original design included a harmonious relationship with God and with others.

God created us to desire that which is good, just, and holy. But from the moment Adam and Eve chose their own plan over God's plan, you and I were powerless to live up to our full potential. Sin corrupted everything. With one decision, longing entered into the world and all sorts of created things were now asked to be more than they were created to be. And even though the power of the Holy Spirit is at work in our lives, we live in a world where sin and evil are at work. Unfortunately, our lives are not immune to the effects of sin, both our own and from others.

I don't know about you, but I'm reminded of this every time I listen to the news. Even now, in my own church, my friends are enduring job losses, miscarriages, divorce, sickness, slander, and division because of political strife and racial hatred. The pain these tragedies stir in my heart reminds me that life shouldn't be this way, but yet—because of sin—it is.

The gap between the life we have and the one we want oftentimes seems unfair. On more than one occasion, I've looked at my own "gap" and said, "Why, Lord? Why does it have to be this way? I don't deserve this!" But in these same moments, he doesn't just leave me to accept the gap with a spirit of resignation. He helps me navigate it, by drawing my heart to remember Jesus, the one who graciously saved me so that one day my hopes for perfection would be realized in eternity with him. And this perfect salvation also includes an eternal justice that will vindicate the times you and I have been wounded by evil and sin in this world.

Ultimately, these seasons of deep longing, where all you can see is the "gap," are opportunities for you to first adjust your expectations. You have an opportunity to take your longing to God himself, laying it at his feet instead of bearing it yourself. This then gives you the freedom to lift your focus off of your situation and place it upon God, trusting that what he has given to you is what he has deemed to be best. And, God's best will always be enough.

The Practice of Self-Examination || Expectations

Remember when I told you in chapter 1 that we'd be learning not just theological ideas, but *applying* those ideas too? Here's where we start. The first spiritual practice that leads us to a place of joy is self-examination. Biblical self-examination is the process by which we make a regular and honest assessment of ourselves through the lens of the gospel. It helps us be aware of how we need to overcome sin and walk in obedience to the Lord. It also helps us uncover the places where we have internalized the false stories of the world. As believers, our greatest goal is to be formed into the image of Christ. Full of grace and free from shame, biblical self-examination helps us intentionally stay true to this commitment to stay aligned to the truth of the gospel.

When I think about this practice, my mind goes back to David, this time in Psalm 139. When we look closely, we see this psalm doing two things: one, it celebrates the character of God, and two, it asks for God to transform the character of David. In Psalm 139:23–24 he writes, "Search me, O God, and know my heart! Try me and know my thoughts! And see if there be any grievous way in me, and lead me in the way everlasting!" With two short verses, David invites God to examine the contents of his heart, correcting any thought or posture that does not align with the Lord's will.

Self-examination helps us push against the cultural current of constant connection with other people. It requires that we get alone with God, pushing pause and assessing how our hearts and lives align with "the way everlasting," or the way that God has designed for us to follow. So, in the moment when we feel our disappointment has lingered a bit too long or is perhaps boiling over into resentment or bitterness or indulgence, our first step is to take a hard look at our expectations. Not only identifying them, but also evaluating if they are prioritizing our comfort or desires over the glory of God.

This is a process that I suggest you do with a journal in prayer. Having a pen and paper with us makes sure we are ready to write down whatever the Lord may reveal. As you reflect on your particular situation, take some time to do these three things:

1. Acknowledge the unmet expectations your longing represents.

Be honest with God and share about the life you wish you had, but don't. Write out your expectations about the life you have and the ways in which you believe they have not been met.

2. Ask the Lord to uncover any unreasonable expectations.

Ask the Holy Spirit to reveal any expectations you hold about your life (or about God) that may not be appropriate—meaning, things you are mad about not having that were never promised to you. Ask him to point out any ways in which your expectations might be rooted in entitlement, fear, or false truth about him or yourself.

3. Ask the Lord to help you surrender to his plan for your life.

As you are praying, ask the Lord, through his Spirit, to give you the wisdom you need to align your expectations with God's Word. Be willing to obey the instructions he gives you. Submit to "walking in the way everlasting," even if his directions don't align with your preferences. God's plan is always better than our plan, even when it doesn't *feel* like it's better.

As hard as this is, here's some good news. Though your pages might be full of heavy emotions or even wet with tears, God does not seek to leave you in this place, but to lead you to a place of comfort and healing. Life is hard, and the longing you feel from unmet expectations can hurt deeply. But your pain doesn't have to last forever. Hope for renewed joy is possible; it just requires you and me to examine our expectations, acknowledge our pain, and embrace the loss (and if you happen to want more on how to embrace loss, just stick with me—that's coming!).

But as we will see with Joshua, this journey toward healing is not one that you have to go on alone. When you are ready to get started, God will be there to help.

Chapter 2

(Don't) Embrace Avoidance

Christmas Eve. That is the day my friend called me and told me the guy I had been dating only a few months before was now getting married to someone else. Our relationship had been rocky, full of miscommunication and unmet expectations. But for most of it I had been in that state of infatuation where your emotions cloud your judgment. I knew we wouldn't work, but in the moment all I could see was how much I cared about him and how much I wanted to be with him. Despite all my prayers and efforts, we ended up breaking up. In his words, he "wasn't ready to get married." Now, as I listened to my friend give me this heartbreaking update, I realized that what he really meant was that he wasn't ready to get married *to me*.

That day I also remember feeling a strange physical sensation in my chest and Googling the phrase, "when your heart feels like it has been hit by a truck." *I didn't even know what I was feeling was heartbreak.* But after reading a few internet articles, I quickly put a name to the cavernous pit that was my empty heart. All at once I became overwhelmed with embarrassment, rejection, anger, and sadness. My response to all this pain was simple—run away. So, for the next year or so, I ran away to the refrigerator and numbed my emotions with food. Lots and lots of food. For most of my life this had been my default response to unwanted emotional pain. I needed to soothe my pain and replenish my joy somewhere, and food has always been such a consistent and faithful option.

But my story is not that uncommon. Well, maybe the whole "he married someone else" part is, but we all have experienced moments of immense emotional pain and heartbreak. Even more so, when life gets to be too hard our immediate reaction is usually to run away. Almost instinctively, we will dedicate the majority of our emotional resources to finding safety, fulfillment, significance, and security outside of the Lord. This means that our hopes for true and lasting joy are usually blocked by one thing—emotional escapism.

In order to experience true joy in the midst of our longing, we have to be willing to face our pain head-on. But many of us don't. Whether consciously or subconsciously, we emotionally run away to *avoid* our pain. Every day we are presented with a buffet of options that are designed to provide us with immediate relief. Things like over-consumption (food/entertainment), physical perfection (ways we obsessively control our bodies), and success (whether at work or in the home) are presented as the soul cure we need. Through TV, music, movies, and social media we are constantly directed to the power of our will as the source of our healing. However, the longer our pain endures, the more and more this buffet of options shows itself for what it is—insufficient and temporary (and sometimes even dangerous or damaging). Emotional escapism will help for a moment, but it's never enough. No amount of money, comfort, control, and attention from others can provide us the healing that only God himself is able to provide. So before we jump back into the life of Joshua, learning how to find joy with God, we must first take a brief detour to talk about the ways we try to find joy without him.

Emotional Avoidance

Have you ever had to carry something heavy far longer than you expected to? Maybe, let's say, luggage you carried on your back for hours and hours during a hiking trip? While the burden itself is taxing, what's worse is that the burden doesn't stay on your back—it starts to impact you all over, even extending to the way you think and the way you treat others in your state of exhaustion or frustration. Your posture changes. Your blood pressure boils. Your thinking turns sour, annoyed, done. You start getting sharp and short with those around you.

Longing can be that way. It usually presents us with situations that come with weighty emotions like grief, anger, and hopelessness. Any of these can seem bearable for a short period of time, but as days turn into months and years, they quickly become too heavy. The physical weight of our emotions is real and affects the entirety of our being. For instance, feelings of hopelessness can infiltrate our minds, creating a downward spiral of negative thoughts. Performing normal, physical functions throughout the day becomes difficult as our hearts and minds are consumed by our pain. Even the way we treat others starts to change. Our burden has gotten so heavy that we can't make room to bear theirs too, and so we get annoyed with their needs, or we constantly consider our burden as worse than theirs—or worse, we don't even notice the weight others are carrying. While pain itself is certainly not a wrong thing to experience in our journey through life (on the contrary, it is to be expected), sometimes it is as if our pain becomes more than a travel companion and ends up in the driver's seat of our lives, controlling our every thought and movement.

Emotional avoidance seeks to relieve us of this weight. We just want to feel happy, hopeful, or normal. Life seems out of sorts, and we just need what has been turned upside down to be turned right side up. So, being the resourceful people we are, we find our own way to satisfy our deepest needs and hopes. We run to the familiar—habits that we have built over a lifetime. While these habitual responses are diverse and many, we could put most of them on a spectrum whose bookends are *obsession* and *denial*.

There are some of us who give a lot of attention to our pain, having no difficulty communicating the longing we are experiencing. Whether it's in our journal, on social media, or in a conversation with a friend, we will tell the stories of our woes and grievances over and over again. We fixate on them. We obsess. Every time a similar situation arises, we relive that painful moment silently in our minds or verbally with others. Now, sharing the truth about our pain is a good and healthy practice. But, being able to retell a story does not result in a resolution of the story, nor does it always help us see the story clearly. On its own, obsessing or retelling the story *ad nauseam* will usually result in us getting emotionally stuck as well as becoming very proficient complainers. No matter how many months or years have passed since the original event, we will live as if it happened yesterday. The pain, always fresh and present on our mind, begins to control how we live and interact with others.

Then there are those of us who outright ignore our pain. We are professional emotion-stuffers who have no problem acting as if nothing in our lives has changed. We hope that if we eliminate the reality of our troubles from our mind, they will simultaneously disappear from our lives. Also, emotions require vulnerability, which some of us view as weakness. For many, signs of weakness are unacceptable; responding in strength is the only acceptable option. So we minimize our emotions or the emotions of others, shutting down conversations that might bring up our pain or denying our pain even exists.

Do you see what's happening in both these cases? Whether our way of avoiding the work of healthily processing our pain comes in the form of obsession or denial, one thing remains the same—our pain is controlling us. Or said another way, whether we obsess over its presence or deny it's even there, the luggage still stays on our back. We're still walking around under its weight. No matter what "flavor" it is, emotional avoidance is a short-term solution that has long-term consequences. Emotional pain does not go away on its own. Left unattended, or perhaps tended to in the wrong ways, it will compound and take root in our soul. Instead of experiencing healing and freedom, we become deeply entangled with emotions that affect the way we live and interact with others. Our methods of avoidance have us trying to find joy and fulfillment on our own, apart from Christ. Whether it's food, shopping, sex, busyness, codependency, or social media, all of our coping mechanisms are many times rooted in our attempts to use created things to give us what only God can provide. They are evidence of our gospel forgetfulness.

Gospel Forgetfulness

Ultimately, as believers, we practice emotional avoidance when we fail to accept and process our emotions in light of the gospel. Now, the gospel is not just a "get-out-of-hell-free card" that tells us how to make it into heaven. It is the good news of redemption for us individually and for the entire world. The gospel tells us the news of how God has redeemed the brokenness of humanity through the life and work of Jesus Christ. This redemption not only has implications for our life after death; it has implications for our life on earth now. As we walk in step with his gospel, God transforms our lived experience on earth as we await eternity with him, and this transformation *includes* our emotions. Only as we live in the truth of the gospel are we able to rightly process the longing we feel.

During my second year in seminary my grandmother died. She had been diagnosed with cancer that previous summer and within seven months the cancer took her life. I don't have words for how hard it was to see my grandmother dete-riorate over those few months. One of the reasons I had moved down to Dallas two years earlier was to be with her, and now she was gone. My grief was overwhelming, appearing in spo-radic, but raging, waves of tears and deep sorrow. Noticing my emotional struggles, a friend invited me to join her for an art class at a local art studio. For the next three months, every week I would spend three hours in a mosaics class, cutting glass and gluing it to a wooden picture frame.

Honestly, the time I spent in that class was so healing for me. Each week I would spend those three hours working on my art project while being present with the Lord in the silence of my pain. Somehow, in that space, the Lord brought heal-ing for my soul. My grief didn't go away completely, but, with the Lord, I was able to process my pain through my art. Now, the Bible doesn't prescribe art classes as the standard way for dealing with the loss of a loved one. But I know enough about the gospel to know that the art wasn't what healed me. For those few months, the gospel helped me to rightly understand my grief, and through that lens I could see how *God* used art to heal my heart and refresh my soul. Why? Because with the precision by which I had to cut and place each tile piece, I was reminded about the precise way in which God made a beautiful world and then followed through with his plans for its restoration, even when sin and suffering turned it ugly. As I was reminded of his faithfulness to restore all of creation, I could confidently trust that he would be faithful to bring beauty from the ashes of my pain. So I grew to expect his character to show up in my life, reminding me of the beauty of my grandmother's life and the hope that, because of her faith, I would see her again in eternity.

I will be the first to say that the truth I clung to in that season of loss, I have quickly forgotten in other seasons. I have forgotten that God is present with me in my pain and that he is better than any coping mechanism I could try to replace him with. For, in the moments I need comfort, he is who true comfort comes from. When I feel unsafe, he is my refuge and protector. When I feel ashamed and embarrassed, he welcomes me with the same love by which he saved me. And, when I feel angry, he is my advocate and avenger. Most of all, his comfort, protection, love, and justice never expire and never fail. But you know what does expire and fail? Our habits of emotional avoidance.

In seasons of longing, when the life we have seems so far away from the life we want, our choice to emotionally live "on the run" reflects a shift in allegiance. In these moments we have chosen to live by the truth of our own "gospel" rather than by the only true gospel of Jesus Christ. We change the story. For starters, we redefine hell. Hell becomes the lack of what we long for—not being married, not having a child, not getting the house or the promotion or the attention. Then we redefine heaven—it becomes a dreamy vision of the marriage, the kids, the house, the promotion, the attention, the success, and so on, with us right there in the center, reveling in the starring role. And to bridge the gap between our personal hell and our personal heaven, we then must come up with some sort of functional, personalized savior to take us from one side to the other. In short, we trust in some other false god to give us what we want, to complete our gospel story. But like I said before, to live by our "gospel" is really another way to describe idolatry because we are choosing created things—idols, functional saviors, false gods, or whatever you want to call them—to give us what only God can provide.

If we were having this conversation in person you might say, "Elizabeth, this seems a bit extreme. I'm just trying to find solace for my soul. I'm not worshiping any idols!" I agree, thinking of our emotional avoidance as idolatry can *seem* a bit extreme. But think about it. Why do you and I run from bringing our longings or our pain (or anything else) to God? Because we think some other god will be better at relieving us from it. In any heavy season, every single one of us naturally goes where we think we'll find relief. And so if we consistently find ourselves at the doorstep of the cupboard, the mall, the app, the ex, and so on, it's clear we believe those are more trustworthy and powerful places to take our pain or desires. We think they will take care of us. Our hearts will take good things and deify them as the center of our lives because we think they will give us the safety, fulfillment, and security we desire.[1] Desperate to regain control of our lives, we run to created things instead of running to God, and this is exactly what the Bible categorizes as idolatry (Jer. 2:13). In the Bible, idolatry is looking to your own wisdom and competence, or to some other created thing, to provide the power, approval, comfort, and security that only God can provide.[2] This means that while our specific habits of emotional avoidance might be different, they functionally have the same root. When we run from bringing our pain, longings, desires, and needs to God (avoidance), we are by default running toward someplace else with those things, somewhere we think is a better place to run (idolatry). Over and over, we forget why *God* is the better place to run.

Remembering the Gospel

So how can we remember? In those impulsive moments that we feel the pull to run from God toward idols, how can we recall that our heart's desires can only be met in Christ? One voice that has greatly influenced my thoughts on this topic is Tim Keller. In his book *Counterfeit Gods,* Keller talks about how our idolatry is really grounded in four key motivational desires: *comfort, approval, power,* and *control.* No matter what our pathway of emotional escape looks like, what we are running toward is most likely the fulfillment of one of these four basic desires. In my own journey of healing, it has been helpful for me to use these categories to identify what has consumed my heart's affections, trust, and loyalty. It also helps me remember the gospel, which reveals why God is the only true source of fulfillment for all the core desires of my heart.

This process of remembering was not invented by Tim Keller, though it comes as no surprise that he has found it, as the wisdom of remembering is woven all throughout Scripture. Throughout the Bible, we are consistently encouraged to see the value of remembrance (Exod. 13:3; Num. 15: 39–40; Deut. 5:15; 6:4–9; 7:18; 8:2, 18; Josh. 1:8, 13; Judges 8:34; 1 Chron. 16:12–1; Esther 9:28; Pss. 1:2; 77:11; John 14:26; 1 Cor. 11:24–25; Eph. 2:11–12; 2 Tim. 2:8). Where the fallenness of

our humanity and the brokenness of our world cultivate limitless opportunities for distraction, Scripture invites us to return
back to what matters. Without shame, it invites us back into
the loving presence of God—our gracious Father who, like the
father in Luke 15, rejoices when we come back "home."

In the spirit of remembrance, I want to use Keller's four
categories to help us uncover the motivational desires that
drive our emotional avoidance. I then want to use the truth
of the gospel to show how our heart's desires can only be met
in Christ.

Comfort

If you idolize comfort, your life is primarily motivated by
a pursuit of pleasure and satisfaction. Freedom, privacy, and
an aversion to stress characterize your equilibrium of calm.
Therefore, when your internal sense of peace has been dis-
rupted, your gut response is to rid yourself of the discomfort
by numbing it. Overconsumption of any kind—food, shopping, illicit substances, sex, or mindless internet scrolling—
provides the immediate feelings of pleasure you deeply desire.
But these sources of comfort never last, leaving you returning
again and again for another temporary boost of happiness.
They also leave residue on our lives, weighing us down with
the long-term consequences of our commitment to their fleeting moments of support.

Where our idol of comfort tells us that indulgence or
pleasure can provide us with peace, safety, and rest, the gospel tells us these things can only be found in Christ. Created
things will never outlast the Creator. You and I were made by

the Lord for his glory. We were *designed* to find our ultimate fulfillment in him. After all, his presence is full of joy and at his right hand are pleasures forevermore (Ps. 16:11). This does not mean that created things cannot and should not bring us joy. What it does mean is that when our pursuit of these things replaces our pursuit of God, any joy we find will be insufficient and lacking. The gospel is the proclamation that our relationship with God has permanently been restored through the work of Jesus Christ. We now have access to an endless supply of comfort, safety, and rest!

Do you seek comfort? Are you constantly turning to worldly sources of pleasure or rest or indulgence in moments of pain? Friend, our God can supernaturally calm the raging waves of our longing and pain. Find your rest in his comfort and peace (Philem. 3–6), for these are the very things Christ died to give you!

Approval

If you idolize approval, your life is primarily motivated by a pursuit of love and respect. Your heart finds security and fulfillment in the affirmation of others. Therefore, when you are seeking an escape from painful emotions, you submerge yourself in your relationships. Now, relationships are a good thing, but when they become an idol to you, you'll find that your constant presence with others is self-seeking, as your actions are motivated by a hope of what you will receive from others rather than what you can give. So, you work to provide *whatever* the relationship needs, even when you lack the capacity or desire to do so. Like all of our idols, the idol of approval slowly requires more and more of us. This means, our fear of rejection will cause us to give all our energy, focus, time, and even money to receive the affirmation we so desperately need. Our relationships will eventually move closer toward codependency as we need the good opinions of others to make us okay inside.

Where our idol of approval tells us that we can find security in the love and affirmation of others, the gospel says we are fully and freely accepted by the Father in Christ. With him, we do not have to sacrifice godliness in order to feel loved and affirmed, nor present a façade in order to stave off rejection. Christ's acceptance is eternal, so unlike man, he will never leave us or forsake us (Heb. 13:5). The gospel reminds us that Christ saved us in spite of our sin. He knows us fully, including the sin we have yet to commit. Our salvation is not based upon our merits or our efforts; it is based on God's grace—the outpouring of his unmerited favor in our lives through the gospel work of his Son.

Do you seek love? Affirmation? Are you constantly wondering how others perceive you? Do you get derailed for weeks if someone misunderstands you or doesn't like you? Friend, God loves and delights in you just as you are. Find your rest in his love and acceptance. In Christ, you have full approval from your Father—yet another thing given to you freely in the gospel.

Power

If you idolize power, your life is primarily motivated by a pursuit of strength and influence over others. You find security in success and recognition, so in the wake of emotional pain, you respond by exerting your influence in the lives of others. This might manifest itself in outbursts of anger, tightening your control over those around you, nitpicking or nagging others, dominating conversations or decisions in group settings, or manipulating situations toward your preferences. Or it might look like becoming withdrawn and withholding acts of vulnerability like forgiveness and trust. Maintaining your posture of strength, you choose self-protection over relational closeness.

Where our idol of power tells us that we can find security in having control over others, the gospel reminds us that all power ultimately rests with God. Any power we think we have is fragile, and our misuse of it is fueled by our insecurity. The gospel reminds us that our influence is to be stewarded for the glory of God. Those around us are not to be used for our personal gain but to be served in humility. In the moments where we feel powerless, humiliated, or unsafe, the gospel shows us that we are secure in Christ and that he alone wields ultimate power in all the right ways.

Do you seek power? Do you find your security in being the best or the one in charge? Do you see your pain as a sign of weakness that you desperately try to hide? Friend, God will not shame us, nor will he ignore the offenses we have endured at the hands of others. Find your rest in his power and, in obedience, care for others with the same grace that God cares for you.

Control

If you idolize control, your life is primarily motivated by a pursuit of complete and unhindered management of your own life. Where the idol of power finds security through controlling others, you find security by trying to control yourself and your environment. Prolonged difficulty comes with a great deal of uncertainty. Even after consistent prayers for clarity and wisdom, the timing by which God will resolve our issue is many times unknown. The weight of knowing your despair might not have an end date is heavy. For those of us who fear uncertainty, this can lead you to grab for any semblance of control you can find. This might manifest itself through overly critical communication, meticulous dieting, obsessive exercise, inflexibility with plans or schedules, being inappropriately strict or punitive with yourself or others, or micromanaging your life and the lives of those around you. Or in order to protect yourself you might withdraw emotionally altogether. But, instead of being fueled by wisdom, these actions are fueled by worry and anxiety. You are trying to provide stability where you believe God has provided none.

Where our idol of control tells us that we can protect ourselves by controlling every aspect of our life, the gospel tells us that God is the only one who has complete control over anything. We as humans are limited in our abilities, but God is limitless. He is all knowing, all powerful, and present everywhere; we are not. Our best efforts at using control to feel secure will leave us in an endless cycle of worry and anxiety, and leave those around us feeling condemned, unloved, and constantly policed. The gospel reminds us that God has not forgotten us and knows what's best for our lives. If he has ensured our *eternal* salvation through Jesus Christ, then he can be trusted to guide us through our *temporary* season of longing.

Do you seek control? Does the uncertainty of your longing cause you worry or stress? Do you try to find peace by making everything and everyone around you bend to your plan? Friend, fight the temptation to think your plan is greater than God's plan. Trust that he really is in control, and more than that, he cares about your worries and will perfectly provide for your needs. Give him the reins, and let him be God. Find your rest in his sovereignty.

As I think about my own journey of healing, I remember the times I reached for comfort or approval to soothe my internal woes. I remember feeling hopeless and unsure of when or how life could get better. The possibility of change seemed so far away that even though I knew it wouldn't last, I chose the path of immediate gratification. I rationalized my behavior by telling myself that at least for a few moments I wouldn't feel my pain.

If time travel was a thing, I would tell my younger self that my impulsive decisions would end up adding to my woes, not relieving them. I would explain how in future years I would have to untangle myself from bad eating habits and codependent relationships. Even though my words might be met with despondency and disbelief (I can be a bit stubborn), my encouragement would be rooted in one small reminder:

"Eventually, Elizabeth, your idols will fail you. But God never will."

In his book *The Deeply Formed Life*, Rich Villodas talks about the need to reframe how we think about the coping mechanisms we use to deal with our pain. His words specifically deal with issues of addiction, but if you read his words, you'll find that they also apply to emotional avoidance.

> Our addiction is our best attempt to survive. Certainly, it leads us down paths of sickness and death, but it is also a signal that we long to live. We just don't know how, apart from this attempt to self-soothe. This is why when helping someone with any kind of addiction, instead of saying "Just stop it. Repent of your sin," we'd do better to say "You've figured out how to stay alive. You've learned how to soothe your pain. But this way doesn't go deep enough. Let's try something else."[3]

Friend, your emotional avoidance is evidence that you are trying to survive in the midst of your longing and pain. You want to live and have figured out a way to function despite the weariness and despair that might be your everyday reality. But while your idols give you the momentary joy or fulfillment you desire, they don't go deep enough. It's time to try something else.

The Practice of Self-Examination ||
Emotional Avoidance

The truth is, our daily temptations toward emotional escapism will not disappear. We will continue to be bombarded with insufficient and temporary options for relief that are imposters of joy. We also have to remember that we have been significantly influenced by our environment (family of origin, friends, faith community, education, work, and the cultural currents of the world around us). Even seemingly inconsequential things are forming us on the inside, whether that be the social media posts we scroll through every day or space we work in or the neighbors we chat with every time we take our dog on a walk. This means that our default responses to difficulty are the outworking of the ways in which we have been shaped by those around us. So, our pathway of healing *requires* that we be honest with ourselves, an honesty that assesses how we are handling hardships of life. It is in this place of vulnerability and transparency that we are able to uncover the lies and misplaced motivations that are directing our choices.

I believe this honesty best comes when we take the time to consider the ways we have allowed idols to capture our affections. Using the practice of self-examination we learned in the previous chapter, we can see the ways in which we have chosen the path of emotional escapism and realign our heart to the truth of God's Word. Over the years the following three questions have helped me to dig deep into the roots of my motivations and better understand the idols that I have looked to for joy.

Question 1: What am I feeling?

The relationship between Christianity and emotions tends to be a bit interesting. For most, we can have a tendency to overemphasize or underemphasize our emotions. Some of us are discipled to believe that our emotional experience with God is the central point of our faith, while others are taught that our emotions are to be suppressed.

Perhaps you grew up on the emotional suppression side of the spectrum. If so, you likely see emotions as irrational, annoying, untrustworthy, or even dangerous. For you, emotions are more of a distraction than an essential part of your humanity, which naturally leads you to minimize your negative emotions. As J. Alasdair Groves and Winston T. Smith write in their book, *Untangling Emotions*, "The driving theological idea here is that negative emotions are inappropriate, given God's sovereignty. If God ordained this suffering to happen and he works all things for good, then the only reason to feel bad is if you don't have enough faith. . . . However, [this] misses that emotions are a God-given gift, an aid in obedience, a constant source for connection with the Lord, and a vital source of information about the deeper problems of our hearts."[4]

In learning to gloss over our deep disappointments with Christianese, we've made our sorrow and godliness mutually exclusive. But as we read through Scripture, faith and sorrow are inextricably connected. Through the stories of the people of God, especially in the Psalms, we see that it's okay to not be okay. But we also see encouragement to bring our brokenness before the Lord.

Therefore, with this first question I encourage you to both name your emotions and validate the freedom you have to feel them. Be as specific as you can. If you feel unsure of what words to use, try some online resources like "the feelings wheel"—these are very helpful in giving you a bigger vocabulary to describe the emotions you may be experiencing.

Question 2: What happened?

After identifying the specific emotion I'm experiencing, this question allows me to pause and think through what might have happened that is causing the emotions I'm feeling. There is always a triggering event that leads us to turn to our default habits of emotional avoidance for refuge. My emotional escapism has been triggered by all sorts of things! It might have been a critical comment from a social media post or the selfishness of a friend. It has also been my grandmother's cancer diagnosis or the suicide of an old roommate. Anything, whether big or small, can be a triggering event.

This question also helps you to see how the event of the moment might be reminding you of a deeper emotional wound. The dishonesty of a spouse hits differently when that spouse has been unfaithful in the marriage. It's as if we are experiencing the original wound all over again. So, by noting the connection, we are able to gain clarity about our emotions but also notice the ways in which we are running away from them.

Question 3: Am I avoiding my pain? If so, how?

This is where you keep it real with yourself! Be honest about what you may be using or doing to avoid feeling the emotions you identified. Have you been doing a bit more shopping, getting more Amazon deliveries than normal? Or maybe you emotionally shutdown every time you have to talk with a certain person or talk about a certain event? Perhaps you've been reaching for the fridge or the phone or the bottle or the ex-boyfriend's number you swore you wouldn't text again?

Resist any shame or embarrassment you might feel. Remember, our emotional escapism is our attempt to survive, and more than that, Christ has taken away our shame—past, present, and future! So, how are you trying to *live* in the midst of prolonged difficulty?

By uncovering the patterns of our emotional escapism, we ultimately reveal the way in which we have placed our hope for salvation in ourselves (or something else) instead of in God. As I've said before, the gospel does not only have implications for eternity, but it has implications for our life now. The good news of salvation through Jesus Christ means that we are invited into eternal relationship with God. In this relationship we have the privilege of experiencing the presence of God in our life. We experience his compassion, power, wisdom, healing, provision, and deliverance. When the emotional weight of life is too heavy to carry, God is there to help, to bear the weight for us. But in order to experience his assistance we have to turn from the idols we have put in his place—we have to name our functional, false saviors and go running back home to the real one. This is why I usually end my time of self-examination in prayer. After having my heart motivations uncovered and brought into the light of the gospel, I am compelled to confess my idolatry to the Lord and repent. I am also compelled to ask for help because it is only in this place of surrender I am able to truly embrace the pain I have been running from.

Friend, it's time to turn from your idols and face— more than that, *feel*—the pain.

But how, you might say? *What does that even mean, and what does it look like?*

Great question.

Chapter 3

Embrace the Loss

I'll be the first one to acknowledge that even though I believe that the events in my life have worked out according to God's gracious and sovereign plan, that truth doesn't immediately make the pain that I *feel* go away. Longing hurts, and sometimes it hurts really bad. A failed marriage, horrible health diagnosis, or prolonged unemployment can leave us feeling a sharp heart pain—or a pain so bad our heart just goes numb. Expectations give birth to a new hope in our lives. When these expectations go unmet, it feels as if hope has died.

Grief is a feeling of deep sorrow that is usually brought on by the significant loss of something or someone. I believe that the deep sorrow of longing is a form of grief, because something we deeply cared about has died. This might be the actual physical death of a loved one, or the death of a relationship, dream, or coveted opportunity. This "death" doesn't mean that this time of grief will last forever, but for many of us, it will last for a while.

In my circle of friends, personality assessments are extremely popular. You might love those, or you may be rolling your eyes right now because you are so over the hype! There are a million versions of them. While people sometimes go a little overboard with them, they've been helpful for me. Especially as I have learned how I'm hardwired to deal with my pain.

According to many personality tests, I'm what you might call a "peacemaker" whose mind is usually in the past. I have a hard time moving forward without resolution. But that doesn't always mean I'm the best at pursuing resolution. What I usually end up doing is simply replaying scenarios and interactions in my head. Over and over and over again. Whenever my mind is at rest or needs an escape from the daily activities of life, I hit rewind and replay things one more time. It's hard for me to move on.

You might not have the same personality type as me, but there's one thing that's true for all of us: our longings shine a light on what our hearts are missing—resolution. The broken relationship doesn't get reconciled; the miracle of healing doesn't come our way; we don't end up getting a new job and remain stuck at the one we hate. In these moments hope can seem so cruel, like a broken slot machine we keep putting coins into, hoping that *this* will be the time we win. But with each attempt the same thing happens—nothing at all.

Grief is hard enough on its own. But in order to experience grief, you have to *acknowledge* that something died. You have to be open to embracing the loss. I don't know about you, but I hate pain and would rather rush past it or avoid it altogether.

But pain is persistent. It won't be rushed and refuses to be ignored. We must face it head-on. All of it.

If you and I are to face our pain, then we need to figure out how to embrace it. The pain of grief is messy, finicky, and a bit of a curmudgeon. It's unpredictable and can go away one day and then come back with a vengeance a few weeks later. Yet, if we can courageously lean into the pain and really *feel* it each time it comes over us in fits and spurts (instead of shoving it down or busying ourselves), then one day, most of it will go away. Little by little, the weight of our sorrow will dissipate, and our hearts will begin to feel joy. Grief doesn't last forever. But in order to move past it, you and I have to be willing to walk through it like Joshua did in that season of mourning, fully embracing the loss we have experienced. Before we can rise up, we have to sit down.

Learning from Joshua

You will have a hard time understanding Joshua 1:1–9 if you don't first read Deuteronomy 34. Honestly, it's a story that requires a reading of the entire Bible up to that point. But this particular passage in Deuteronomy helps us understand the appropriateness of the words that God says to Joshua. By way of reminder from what we've explored in chapter 2, in Joshua 1:2, God says "Moses my servant is dead. Now therefore arise . . ." At first glance this comment might seem a bit insensitive, but God is not telling Joshua he just needs to "get over" Moses's death. If we look back at Deuteronomy 34 to fill in some details for us, we see what happened in the space between Moses's death and Joshua's call—Israel mourned Moses's death. "And the people of Israel wept for Moses in the plains of Moab thirty days. Then the days of weeping and mourning for Moses were ended" (Deut. 34:8). Instead of ignoring their grief or running from it, Israel, as a community, set aside time—an entire month—to mourn the death of their beloved leader.

Outlined by the Laws in the Torah, Jewish mourning practices provided an outlet for grief and a means by which the life of the deceased could be honored and respected.[1] These laws outlined how the bereaved should dress, eat, and conduct themselves in the days and weeks after the death of their loved one. Jewish tradition recognized the hard realities of loss and grief, and provided structured and clear pathways by which these emotions could be expressed. Hardwired into these cultural practices was the belief that life does not continue as normal after a death has occurred. In order to move forward, one must process their grief through mourning and lament.

Don't miss this, friend! God gave Joshua time to embrace his loss. He doesn't just tell him to get over it, or overload him with other activities so that he'll be distracted. No, through this practice of lament God gave Joshua time to navigate the sorrow, disappointment, and despair he must have felt.

Lament

Suffering is an invitation to lament to God.[2] Instead of holding the weight of our emotional pain or running from it, God invites us to bring it to him. Communicated through a posture of prayer, lament pours out our fears, frustrations, and sorrows to God.[3] It is the honest cry of a weary soul, who in vulnerability and weakness surrenders its sorrows to a sovereign God. Yet, while it might bubble up from a place of despair, lament is not a hopeless prayer. In fact, it is pregnant with hope and steeped in rich theological truth. To lament is to ask God to intervene in our situation. But we only ask God to intervene because we believe he can and will. To pray this kind of prayer requires that we relinquish control over the situation, acknowledging our limitedness. Though, while we have limits, God does not. Lament stands on the fullness of God's character and demands for his character to be made manifest in our lives.

In Scripture, the people of God are no strangers to the process of lament. Scattered throughout the pages of the Bible are prayers of lament, so much so, that there are more psalms of lament than psalms of praise. These prayers tell the story of suffering, unmet expectations, and extended seasons of longing. David's sin and the afflictions of his children, the destruction of Jerusalem, the death of Lazarus, and Jesus's impending crucifixion all find themselves the subject of a prayer of lament (2 Sam. 18; Pss. 51; 79; Matt. 26:36–46; John 11:17–32). These expressions of pain were not composed; they were raw, full of passionate explanations of sorrowful situations and even accusations against God. As you read through each prayer it becomes apparent that, for them, suffering was a familiar companion, but so was the faithful presence of God.

Israel had been chosen by God. While they were slaves in Egypt, there were other people living all over the world—in Europe, Asia, Africa, and North America. But God specifically showed up in their situation, using them as the means through which he would bless the world (Gen. 12:1–3). Israel had seen God miraculously deliver them out of slavery. They had also seen God commit himself to them through the Mosaic covenant. A people who had felt abandoned and lost was now told they were fully accepted and safe.

Furthermore, the interconnectedness of humanity and the divine was a common reality at this time in the world. Whether people were worshiping idols or the one true God, there was an understanding that life was controlled by the hand of the divine. So, Israel's way of life was deeply shaped by their trust in God's sovereignty. There was no question that he would protect and provide for them. He had promised he would, and God never breaks his promises.

It is for this reason that Israel brought their pain before God through prayers of lament. In his book *Rejoicing in Lament*, Todd Billings speaks to this connection when he says, "It is precisely out of trust that God is sovereign that the psalmist repeatedly brings laments and petitions to the Lord. . . . Because of their faith in God's sovereignty, the psalmists have high expectations of God; because they take God's promises seriously, they lament and protest when it seems that God is not keeping his promises."[4] Israel's relationship with God included the expectation that he would not only care about them in their moment of distress, but that he would show up and fix it. Some way, somehow, God could provide a soothing balm for their pain.

You can see this dynamic in the Psalms when the biblical authors use phrases like:

- "Why do you forget us forever, why do you forsake us for so many days?" (Lam. 5:20).
- "Help me, O LORD my God! Save me according to your steadfast love!" (Ps. 109:26).
- "To you, O LORD, I call; my rock, be not deaf to me, lest, if you be silent to me, I become like those who go down to the pit" (Ps. 28:1).

In each prayer the expression of lament is connected to God's promise of covenantal faithfulness. It is as if the psalmist is saying, "Where are you, God? I'm hurting. You said you would be here, but I can't feel your presence!"

As a people who experienced slavery, war, and the conquest of foreign lands, Israel understood suffering to be a part of life. They knew what it was to experience death, defeat, and loss. But instead of avoiding it, they were a people who embraced their loss. Through mourning and lament they were able to honor the lives that had been lost and in doing so honor the God from whom those lives came. Their lament was grounded in a deep submission to God's sovereignty, but their submission was not blind. In moments of despair, when it seemed as if God was not upholding his promises of love and faithfulness, Israel brought their pain to him. They knew that God's responsibility for their well-being meant that he was also responsible to care for them in their pain.

Why We Don't Lament

When we look at Israel's natural and necessary pathway to healing, it feels foreign to many of us. We are unacquainted with the practice of lament, unsure of how to bring our cries of pain and outrage to God. Why? Of many things, there are three primary things that keep us from it—discomfort, fear, and anger.

Discomfort

Suffering makes us uncomfortable because we have failed to normalize its recurring presence in our lives. We don't expect to experience suffering but see it as an interruption in our progressive pursuit of an easy life. The American Dream, the undercurrent of our culture, tells us that if we work hard, life will eventually get better. This story of triumphalism has shaped us in such a way that our expectations for life do not include the possibility of suffering, especially suffering that is prolonged and painful.

This dynamic has made its way into the way we understand and express our faith. While our discipleship environments might provide space for *moments* of sorrow, we mostly focus our time on moving past the pain to get to our deliverance and praise. Now, I will be the first to say that there is nothing wrong with us being a people of praise! However, Scripture shows us that life with Christ includes both praise and lament, and our overemphasis on the former has weakened our ability to participate in the latter. This rush to find relief makes us uncomfortable in the presence of suffering and unsure of how to provide comfort, filling the awkward silence of suffering with spiritual platitudes or escapism. Our lack of familiarity with lament has caused our theology of suffering to become shallow.

Suffering also makes a previously stable life unstable. This instability leads us to immediately look for a source of safety and security, something in which we can place our trust. Spiritual platitudes offer quick but short-lasting stability. While statements like "God will provide," "God will do a miracle," or "God works all things together" are true, they fail to come with the needed support for when those statements are not immediately realized. Because, sometimes the provision doesn't come in the way we wanted it to. Sometimes we don't see the miracle. Sometimes everything falls apart. That's the nature of prolonged suffering. The resolutions to our issues are far away or they never come.

On the other hand, spiritual platitudes can provide simple answers for complicated problems. Yes, we know that God works all things together, but in the midst of trauma like sexual abuse, domestic violence, or death, those statements seem insensitive and insufficient. Sometimes suffering doesn't make sense and to try to rationalize it causes more damage.

I can't count how many times someone has tried to explain the reason for their singleness or the singleness of another person. Regardless of what we may think, no one is ready to get married and plenty of messed-up people have beautiful weddings. There is no consistent matrix by which one person gets the desire for marriage fulfilled in their life and another person does not. But people try to come up with answers anyway.

They try to make sense of something that doesn't make sense. It usually results in an answer that is some version of "God is withholding this from you because something is wrong with you. Once you fix it, you'll get married." Instead of being okay with the ambiguous in-between space of pain, we make people, or ourselves, believe that suffering and blessing are merit-based. With this logic, we suffer because something is wrong with us and are blessed because we are living right. In believing this we paint God to be someone he is not—transactional and unconcerned with our pain.

The truth is, God does not just move past our pain or offer us simple answers. Many times, he does not lift the discomfort. He sits in it with us. I think of the story of Lazarus in John 11. Even though Jesus knew he would soon raise Lazarus from the dead, he still wept over the death of his friend. I want to believe his tears expressed the pain he was feeling for the loss of Lazarus, but also for the pain Lazarus's sisters had experienced. Jesus had not just come to do a miracle and then go home. For that moment, albeit brief, Jesus was present with Mary and Martha in their pain. And in the same way he is with us.

In the weariness that prolonged suffering can bring, God is there with us, patiently sitting with us in our sadness. The God of the universe doesn't give us shallow answers or spiritual platitudes. He understands the depth of sorrow we experience and offers us his comforting presence.

Lament helps us handle our discomfort by being present with the Lord. It is the prayer for folks in the in-between space, whose situations do not have easy answers or quick resolutions. Lament grounds our sorrows in a truth-filled hope that reminds us that our pain is not lost on God. He knows, he cares, and he's there with us in it.

Friend, when your pain makes you uncomfortable, don't run from it. Be present with the Lord in it. Resist the temptation to find solace in easy answers and find security in stability of God's character, specifically his love and faithfulness. Trust that he will provide the support you need, even when he doesn't provide the answers you want.

Fear

Like discomfort, fear is another reason why we do not practice lament. To be specific, we fear that lament won't work and that we will be left in our pain. Lament requires honesty and courage. We have to be honest about our pain and have the courage to hope that God will do something about it. But honesty requires a great deal of vulnerability, uncovering a wounded heart we have fought so hard to protect. Self-protection is the gut instinct that makes us run to our idols. Even though they are terribly insufficient, we trust in their false promises of protection. Lament requires us to take down our walls of defense and uncover our wounds before the Lord. But to be open is to be vulnerable to disappointment, and for an already weary heart, disappointment can be devastating.

Any life that has been strapped with suffering for an extended period of time has experienced a considerable amount of disappointment. While sometimes because of inappropriate expectations, this disappointment is often the fruit of rightly placed hopes going unrealized. It's the cancer treatment that doesn't work or the arguments that don't cease even after seeing multiple marriage counselors. The pain of prolonged suffering is unique in that most times, prayers have already been offered for the situation. We've already asked God to intervene and maybe asked our spiritual community to pray that same thing for us. But, even with fervent committed prayer, the outcome we hope for sometimes doesn't happen. With each disappointment, our hope is seemingly dashed upon the rocks as it becomes harder and harder to hope.

As a black woman I often think about the faith of my ancestors. Enslaved for hundreds of years and the recipients of horrific and inhumane treatment for many years thereafter, they found strength in lament. As a people we have seen change and freedom, but that change did not come quickly. Yet, my people held fast to their faith in God and found strength in approaching him with the same honesty that we see from the story of Israel in Scripture.

Much of the lament of black Christians has historically been communicated through song. Our Negro spirituals captured the emotional weight of a broken people, but a broken people who chose to keep hoping. As author Jemar Tisby wrote in his book *The Color of Compromise*, "the Negro spiritual put black lamentations into songs that soared upward as prayers for God to save them and grant them perseverance to exist and resist."[5] These songs were prayers deeply rooted in the truth of Scripture, as they called out against the evils of slavery and prayed for justice and deliverance.

He deliver'd Daniel from the lion's den,
Jonah from the belly of the whale,
And the Hebrew children from the fiery
furnace
And why not a every man.

I set my foot on the Gospel ship
And the ship it began to sail,
It landed me over on Canaan's shore
And I'll never come back any more.

Didn't my Lord deliver Daniel,
Deliver Daniel deliver Daniel.
Didn't my Lord deliver Daniel,
And why not a every man?[26]

I believe my ancestors' need for God was greater than their fear. Like Israel, I believe they had a deep dependence on God, cultivated by their unwavering belief in his sovereignty and faithfulness. They prayed the words of Psalm 13:1 and Isaiah 40:31, for theirs was a weariness that petitioned God for both his intervention and persevering strength.

Yet, another part of what made these songs so impactful was their ability to allow a community to share in their laments together. When one person might have been unable to muster up the strength themselves, the verbal and visual testimony of others served as a reminder that lament truly did have the power to uplift and heal. Hope is contagious and in moments of despair, the verbal cries of others to God can give us strength enough to cry out to God ourselves.

While we might have to adjust our expectations for hope, there is always hope. In the same way that lament reminds us of the compassionate presence of God, lament reminds us of God's patience with our emotional fragility. Repeated disappointment makes us fragile, giving us hearts that easily break because they have been weakened by the brokenness of life. God knows this. He knows you are hesitant to trust him and are emotionally weary. He knows you think it's more costly to hope in him than it is to run from your pain. You also aren't the first believer to experience this. So in the same way that he has given Christians of years past power to endure, he will do the same for you. When our fear tells us that God isn't trustworthy or that he won't care for us, lament reminds us that he does.

Anger

Lastly, the third reason some of us don't bring our pain to God is because we are angry with him. Seeing him as responsible for the wounds we carry, we don't know how or don't feel comfortable bringing our full force of our unadulterated anger to him. As I like to say, we don't think we can *keep it real* with God.

Our expectations about life include expectations about what God will and won't do for us. To believe that God is sovereign is to believe that he is in complete control of everything. Nothing happens in this world that he does not allow. So, in our mind, God, being good, would naturally give us everything that is good and withhold everything that is evil. Deeply embedded in all of our expectations is the belief that a good God will not allow bad things to happen to his people. That means when bad things happen to us or we don't receive the good we believe we deserve, we feel like God has not held up his end of the bargain.

Anger is an emotional response to injustice, real or perceived. To be angry with God is to believe that he has done something unjust. Problem is, God is never unjust. He never does anything wrong, but exists in eternal perfection. It is true that someone or something is to blame for the trouble in our life. But that blame never rests on God.

We suffer trouble because of our own sin, the sin of others, the brokenness of the world, and the attacks of the enemy. In all these situations God has the ability to intervene. Sometimes he does and sometimes he doesn't. This is the flip side to his sovereignty. Yes, God is in complete control but he also gets to decide how he exerts that control in this world. As created beings, we won't always understand or agree with what God allows in our lives.

Friend, there will never be sufficient answers for the pain you and I experience in this life. In our life with Christ we have to trust he knows best. But, in order to get to this place of trust we have to be honest with God about our anger. To find the healing we desire, we have to bring to him the very expectations we feel he has forgotten, mishandled, and ignored.

The book of Job is about suffering. Right at the beginning of the story, seemingly overnight, Job's life falls apart. God himself declared Job to be a righteous man. But this did not prevent him from losing his children, his wealth, and eventually his health. Seeking to comfort him in his suffering, Job's friends and his wife offered the same response many of us have heard: "What did you do to deserve this, Job?! Suffering only happens to those who do bad things." Job himself starts to use that same argument in his response to God. Page after page we are introduced to the all-too-familiar expectations that both Job, his wife, and his friends have about suffering and God.

Then God shows up. Honestly, he shows up and shuts Job down! In Job 38:2–7 God says,

> "Who is this that darkens counsel by words
>   without knowledge?
> Dress for action like a man;
> I will question you, and you make it known
>   to me.
> "Where were you when I laid the foundation
>   of the earth?
> Tell me, if you have understanding.
> Who determined its measurements—surely
>   you know!
> Or who stretched the line upon it?
> On what were its bases sunk,
> or who laid its cornerstone,
> when the morning stars sang together
> and all the sons of God shouted for joy?"

For the next few chapters, God basically tells Job, "Who are you to tell me what I should do? Last time I checked, I'm God and you are not." Through all his pointed questions, God makes Job reckon with the fullness of what it means for him to be God. But take note of *when* God shows up in the

conversation. There are only forty-two chapters in the book
of Job, and God shows up at chapter 38. For thirty-seven
chapters we hear Job and his friends talk about his suffering.
In particular, we see Job freely express his anger to God. The
first few words in Job 38:1 say this: "Then the LORD answered
Job." What does that tell us? That God has been listening the
whole time.

What we find in the first thirty-seven chapters of Job is
his lament. He freely brings his anger and accusations to God.
But, by the time you get to the end of the story it becomes
clear that Job's perspective has changed. In Job 42:2–6 he says
to God,

> "I know that you can do all things,
> and that no purpose of yours can be
>   thwarted.
> 'Who is this that hides counsel without
>   knowledge?'
> Therefore I have uttered what I did not
>   understand,
> things too wonderful for me, which I did not
>   know.
> 'Hear, and I will speak;
> I will question you, and you make it known
>   to me.'
> I had heard of you by the hearing of the ear,
> but now my eye sees you;
> therefore I despise myself,
> and repent in dust and ashes."

Job's expectations about God have been adjusted, with his anger being transformed into reverence and submission. But this transformation would not have happened if Job had kept his anger to himself, bottling it up or simply walking away from the Lord. It was *through* his lament—*thirty-seven* chapters of it—that he was able to wrestle with God, speaking the truth about his frustration and resentment. But it was also in that place of lament that his expectations for life with God could be adjusted and his hope in God reaffirmed.

Friend, God is not afraid of your anger, nor will you dishonor him by bringing it to him. He already knows, and welcomes you to engage with him, not run from him. It may take one chapter in some seasons or thirty-seven in others, but lament always allows us to be honest with God and take the first step toward experiencing the healing our hearts desire.

The Practice of Lament

For most of this chapter, I have been trying to convince you of the value and necessity of lament in your walk with the Lord. Seasons of prolonged suffering produce emotional longing whose weight is too great for any of us to bear alone. Rather than turn to our idols of comfort, approval, power, and control, Scripture calls us to turn to God through lament. He understands the depth of our pain, seeks to care for the fragility of our hearts, and is not judging us for the messiness or intensity of our emotions. He is not offended by any of it, but invites us to bring it *all* to him.

The prayers of lament we read in Scripture prove to be a consistent model for how we can bring our cares before the Lord. Each prayer tends to have a similar rhythm, with the author flowing through several different movements of expression as he makes his concerns known to the Lord. While providing an intimate glimpse into the author's anguish and despair, these prayers also provide consolation as we see the author's words produce fruit in the form of hope and joy.

If you know anything about the life of David, you know that it is fraught with struggle and difficulty. Whether it's the years he spent running for his life from Saul or the devastating aftermath of his sinful actions with Bathsheba, to say David's life was hard is an understatement. Much of our understanding about these situations comes through the prayers of lament that he wrote in the book of Psalms. As we read through the psalms, we gain an intimate view of the prolonged suffering David experienced throughout his life.

Of all the lament prayers I've read though, David's prayer in Psalm 13 sticks out the most for me. I believe it serves as a beautiful example, demonstrating a three-step progression of lament and showing us what it looks like to embrace our pain and find hope in the midst

of sorrow. I'll include it here below, so that as we walk
through it, you can see the way it unfolds:

> ¹How long, O Lord? Will you forget
>   me forever?
>   How long will you hide your face
>   from me?
> ²How long must I take counsel in my
>   soul
>   and have sorrow in my heart all the day?
>   How long shall my enemy be exalted
>   over me?
> ³Consider and answer me, O Lord my
>   God;
>   light up my eyes, lest I sleep the sleep
>   of death,
> ⁴lest my enemy say, "I have prevailed
>   over him,"
>   lest my foes rejoice because I am
>   shaken.
>
> ⁵But I have trusted in your steadfast
>   love;
>   my heart shall rejoice in your
>   salvation.
> ⁶I will sing to the Lord,
>   because he has dealt bountifully
>   with me.

1. Tell Him

In Psalm 13:1–2, David expresses how he feels abandoned by God. Four times, he repeats the phrase "How long," revealing his frustration over the extent of God's absence. In his mind, he is overcome by his enemies while God is nowhere to be found. David's words are honest, direct, and unhurried. It is as if he throws his cares to the Lord, seeking to release the weight of sorrow his soul has been carrying.

Lament provides us the opportunity to *keep it real* with God. Be honest about what has happened and how you feel about it. Tell God about your hopelessness, sadness, and weariness. Share about the ways in which you feel abandoned or overwhelmed by your situation. Remember, the longing in our hearts represents a grief of sorts, as our hope for a specific reality has died. In order to embrace our pain, we have to acknowledge it. Lament allows us to openly and honestly express the loss we feel to God. Whether it is from the pain of prolonged singleness or the burden of caring for an aging parent, crying out to God allows us to fully process our grief in a space where we are known and loved.

2. Ask Him

The entirety of Psalm 13 is grounded in David's beliefs about God's character and nature. He cries out to God because he believes God can actually change his situation. He also knows that God is committed to him based on the Lord's repeated promises to provide for his good. So in verses 3–4, we see David empowered by these truths to fearlessly ask God for deliverance.

Our longing represents situations in life that we wish would change—situations we are powerless to change on our own. Yet in our lament we are reminded that what seems impossible to us is possible for our God. Our relationship with God is one grounded in covenantal promise by which we can and should confidently petition him to intervene in our lives. We ask with open hands, believing that God will show up in our situation, even though we don't have all the details for when and how.

3. Trust Him

David ends Psalm 13 with a declaration of praise. But his praise is not for what God will do. It is for what he has already done. In verses 5–6, David talks about how he will sing God's praises because the Lord has "dealt bountifully" with him in the past. He trusts God now because of how God has previously delivered him. In spite of his pain, David chooses to praise God for the many ways he has already blessed him.

Grounded in the faithfulness of God, lament leads us to end our prayers remembering what God has previously done in our lives. As we recount the moments when God did bring unexpected provision in the very moment we needed it, a certain calm comes over us. Remembering the past goodness of God helps us trust that we will experience his goodness in the future. We serve a God who gave his life for us that we might spend eternity with him. If we can trust him to care for our salvation, then we can trust that he will care for *all* of our needs.

As I write this, our world is fighting through a global pandemic. When I think about what this disease has done to our world—all the people who have died, businesses that have closed, and people who languished physically and emotionally in isolation, I feel such a heavy weight of grief. But I also know that I'm not the only one grieving; the whole world is.

While I was talking to friends about this global pain, one suggested that we needed to lament. She said we needed to corporately bring our pain to the only one who can provide us comfort, healing, and hope, because our corporate pain is too great to be sustained by temporary and insufficient coping mechanisms. In these few words, my friend reminded us all that we needed something, or better yet, *Someone* stronger to meet us in the deep valleys of our grief.

Friends, lament connects us to that Someone, helping us trust that God's past blessings will extend into both our present and future realities. Even if it's not until eternity, lament helps us trust that one day our God will make all things right. But simultaneously, lament stirs something in us. It births in us a small seed whose glimmering light of resilience pushes us to keep walking, fueled by the belief that someway, somehow, we will "see the goodness of the LORD in the land of the living" (Ps. 27:13 NIV).

Where does lament lead us?

To the next stop on our journey: hope.

Chapter 4

Embrace Hope

I met Sylvia at a conference. I had been invited to lead a few sessions interviewing specific people, and Sylvia was one of those people. During my time in ministry there have been a few different events or moments that have shaped me significantly, and my interview with Sylvia is one of them.

She was a church executive, in her sixties, and single—never married. Our discussion focused on life in unexpected places, so naturally we talked about her life as a single woman. Sylvia was so honest, the kind of honest that happens in a conversation between friends and not on a stage in front of hundreds of people. She spoke about the sorrows and joys of her season and helped shed light on the ways that singles are overlooked and undervalued in the church. But what stood out to me about our conversation was what she said at the very end. In my last question to her I asked, "Knowing what you know now, what advice would you give to a younger thirty-something, Sylvia?" She flipped the script and directed her answer right to me! Sylvia said, "I would tell *you* to keep on praying for marriage if you desire it, don't settle, and if you get to be my age and are still single, know that you will be okay!"

As she said that last point, it took everything in me to keep from crying. The idea of spending another thirty years unmarried stirs up my feelings of emotional longing. I think there is this fragile sense of optimism singles have that one day their longing will go away. One day marriage will come and what is hard about life won't be hard anymore. On the other side of that optimism is something that many singles can't even fathom—the idea that they may never get married. For them, a life that includes the constant companionship of their longing is unbearable. But Sylvia's words entered into that place of weightiness and lightened the load of the pain.

When she said "you will be okay," she didn't mean that my life would be perfect or that I wouldn't experience sorrow anymore. I believe Sylvia was letting me know that in spite of my pain, my life would still be blessed, full, and fruitful. With four simple words Sylvia gave me hope.

Lament Births Hope

Lament is the language of the dark night of the soul. In his grace, God gives us this space to bring our worries and concerns before him. It is a place where he invites us to linger, unhindered and unhurried. If that place scares you, here's the good news about it: it's not all darkness and despair. It includes hope too. Because there is no lament without hope; they are inextricably intertwined. As we bring our sorrows before the

Lord, we stand upon the implications of his sovereignty. We speak with the belief that our words will reach the ears of a God who will respond. It is in the midst of this belief that hope resides.

However, even though we can know where it resides and from who it comes, it can be hard to understand the exact substance of hope. While sometimes confused with optimism, hope is more than a simple sentiment. It is not naive, unaware of the truth about our situation. The nature of prolonged suffering includes the possibility that our situation may not change for a long period of time. So, in order to sustain us, hope must be grounded in something outside of us that is unwavering. It must be linked to a reality that is true whether we feel hopeful or not.

Sylvia's words to me were supported by more than sixty years of wisdom. Knowing all of what could, and probably would, cause me pain in my own journey of singleness, she still was convinced that there was hope for me. Far from naive, the hope she gave me is similar to the hope we see emerge in the life of Joshua. It was linked not to a husband, but to a reality that has been in motion since the beginning of time.

Learning from Joshua

At the moment that God tells Joshua to arise, he is drawing him, and the people of Israel, out of their time of mourning and lament. After giving them time to process the loss of Moses, God tells Joshua, "Moses my servant is dead. Now therefore arise, go over this Jordan, you and all this people,

into the land that I am giving to them, to the people of Israel"
(Josh. 1:2). What God instructs Joshua to do presents a marker
in time, a turning point in the story of the people of Israel.
God was taking Israel from the wilderness, through the Jordan
River, into the land of promise.

Crossing a large body of water. Does that sound familiar?
Of course it does! This movement through the Jordan River
is reminiscent of another time in which Israel crossed over
a major body of water. As you likely remember, after being
delivered out of slavery, God brought Israel through the Red
Sea. It was a miracle that signified a transition of power, a
final release of Israel from the oppressive rule of Egypt into
the care of God. The crossing of the Red Sea signaled a new
beginning for Israel that included receiving the land that God
had promised to their forefather Abraham.

Wonderful. A new, free season in the land of promise on
the other side of all that despair. But, as you probably remember, there's a plot twist: the land was inhabited by lots of different people groups who were stronger than Israel. Faced with
overwhelming feelings of fear, Israel, almost unanimously,
voted against taking the land that God had given them.
Rather than fearing the unlimited power of God, Israel feared
their own limitedness. This disbelief in God's ability to make
good on his word had postponed their entrance into the promised land. For forty years they had wandered in the wilderness,
fighting to be obedient and trust the faithfulness of God,
until all who had failed to believe had died. Then, with a new
generation, God would bring Israel to the shores of the Jordan
River for a second chance at their new beginning.

Now, this transition into the promised land did not bring Moses back to life. Nor did it relieve any remaining grief that Joshua or Israel may have been feeling. Most likely, those feelings would persist for a long time. But in the midst of their pain, God continued moving them forward to the fulfillment of his promises. He didn't get distracted, discouraged, or lost. God remained steadfast, upholding promises that were made not just to Israel, but to Abraham, and even to Adam and Eve. While Israel was experiencing emotional loss, grief, and sadness, God was still at work. No matter how deep their pain was, they could trust that he was always doing a *new thing*. But if they were not careful, Israel's hope in God could get consumed by the enemy of hope—doubt and despair.

The Enemy of Hope

Words are my art. So, whether writing or speaking I am always trying to get better at my craft. One of the ways that I do this is by listening to or reading the words of other people. There is one pastor who I listened to constantly while I was in seminary. Honestly, his preaching helped me get through seminary! Whew! As I would listen to him, I would try to pinpoint what made him so good. Every artist has strengths, things that make their work unique and beautiful. Other than teaching the Bible really well, what made this particular pastor's work beautiful was his transparency, humor, and phenomenal ability to tell stories.

This brotha could tell a good story! He pulled them from his own life and from the countless books he read. From the amount of stories he used, I feel like he read all the time! Since I was listening to learn about Jesus *and* observe the beauty of the art he created with words, I paid attention to the books he would quote. Out of all the sermons I listened to, the one I heard him use the most was *The Pilgrim's Progress.*

Written in 1678 by John Bunyan, *The Pilgrim's Progress* is an allegory of the spiritual journey of Christians. It chronicles the tale of a man named Christian who makes a journey from the City of Destruction (Earth) to the Celestial City (heaven). Throughout the story, the main character Christian encounters lots of hardship and difficulty. Bunyan uses the characters and situations in his story to communicate deep truths about the life of the believer. One such incident is when Christian and his travel companion, Hopeful, get caught up by a Giant whose name is Despair.

During their journey, Christian and Hopeful wander onto the Giant's property. Upon finding these trespassers, the Giant promptly throws them into a dungeon in his Doubting Castle. For days the Giant deprives them of food and subjects them to merciless mental and physical abuse. At one point he tells Christian and Hopeful their situation is so bad that their best option would be to take their own lives. Hopeful ends up intercepting this horrible advice and, living up to his name, provides Christian with several reasons for why listening to the Giant would be foolish. But ruthlessly persistent, the Giant Despair comes back and gives them another mental and physical beatdown. Once again he tells Christian and Hopeful that their situation won't get any better. He tries to convince them that, for them, showing up for life is a waste of time.

Each morning presents us with the same challenge—showing up for life. We are given the opportunity to be fully engaged with the life God has given us, seeing each moment as an opportunity to love him, humanity, and his creation. We move throughout the day empowered by the light of his glory and presence. But when life is hard, suffering can hover over us like a cloud of darkness. It blocks the light and drains our joy. What used to be easy is now hard. The weight of suffering is heavy, and in the moments we are not running from our pain or lamenting it, we can be overtaken by it.

Like the Giant in *The Pilgrim's Progress*, despair is a powerful storyteller. In moments of suffering, it can pop up in our minds and slowly craft an enticing narrative. With a quiet persistence, this slow drip of hopelessness reframes how we view the world. It will teach us to view life through the lenses of negativity and cynicism. The life that was once full of vibrant opportunity now seems to be a burden. What used to have purpose, now seems to be a waste of time.

Furthermore, despair usually stirs up doubt. When our optimism has been met with the harsh truths of reality, we can start to wonder whether what we thought was true is still true. Doubt builds like a small funnel cloud until it feels like a tornado is whipping through our minds. Where we were once clear about the goodness of God, we are now confused. Have you ever felt that way? I know I have. In my own moments of doubt, my mind is usually filled with questions that I will respond to using any of the following answers: *"It won't work out. You aren't worth it. You don't deserve it. Just give up!"*

In order to fully understand hope, we have to understand doubt and despair. Seeing the depths to which our hearts and minds will fall shows us the power and strength of what is needed to pull us back up. Despair shows us that in order to not just survive but thrive amid our suffering, we need a new story. Our minds need to be reframed to resist the unrelenting downward pull of despair. The truth of hope has to be an unwavering story that is strong enough to punch through the dungeons that despair tries to lock us in. It needs to provide a way for us to break out and stay free.

Thankfully, *The Pilgrim's Progress* does not end with Christian and Hopeful left in the dungeon. While reeling from the Giant's final attack, Christian remembers he has a key called Promise that will open any lock in Doubting Castle. He then proceeds to take this key and open every door in the castle until he and Hopeful are able to escape.

After reading this story for the first time, my initial thought was, *How did he not lose that key after being beat up so many times?!* Christian and Hopeful had been in that dungeon for days. They had walked around with the Giant taking them outside for a "scared straight" field trip to the graveyard! Yet in spite of all this movement and activity, Christian never lost the key. It stayed with him the entire time, even in the moments he forgot it was there.

Obviously, the name of the key is symbolic. Bunyan meant for Christian's key to represent the promises of truth that are designed to set people free. Specifically, the key represents the truth of the gospel—the truth of what God is doing in us and through us because of what he has done *for* us. Even when we forget it, it's there. And it can get us through anything.

The Object of Our Hope

Friend, while hope is the fruit of lament, the substance of our hope is God himself. He is the only one who is unchanging and strong enough to overcome the power of doubt and despair in our life. But our hope in him is not something we muster up by the sheer strength of our will. In the words of Kathleen O'Connor, "Biblical hope does not emerge from proper reasoning or new information. It is not optimism or wishful thinking. It is not a simple act of the will, a decision under human control, or a willful determination. It emerges without clear cause like grace, without explanation, in the midst of despair."[1] This mysterious and miraculous appearance of hope in our lives is a gift from God by the power of the Holy Spirit.

Far from being simply an emotional sentiment, God's gift of hope is the ability to believe in him. It is a gift of the gospel, a deep benefit that overflows out of the work of salvation that he has accomplished on our behalf. Hope moves us to believe that God is not going to leave us in our pain, but is doing a work of transformation in and through it. The moment in which we might be overcome by despair, hope reminds us that God is both aware and concerned about our pain. It assures us that in our lowest moments, he will remember us and not leave us empty-handed. But in order to see such a blessing rightly, we have to have a right understanding of the work of transformation God is doing.

God's Plan of Restoration

From the opening pages of Scripture, we are told that God created the world in glorious and beautiful perfection. But this peaceful utopia was soon invaded by an intruder—sin. In the pages that follow, story after story reveals the chaos, destruction, and brokenness sin has caused. But these same stories tell us that our God is aware of this brokenness and is working right now to fix it. In Genesis 3:15, God promises Adam and Eve that one day he will make right all that went wrong—that he will do a new thing, restoring all that is broken in the world.

For thousands of years, God continually reaffirms this promise to his people, all while meeting their daily needs. Whether its protection or provision, God consistently gives his children the help and healing they need to live life well. He is steadfast and faithful, committed to bringing his children, and this world, to the goal he promised way back in the garden of Eden.

In spite of their brevity, the first few words of Matthew prove to be some of my favorite words in Scripture. Why? Because Matthew 1:1 announces the fulfillment of God's Genesis 3:15 promise. This first verse of the New Testament is an announcement of the birth of Jesus; the salvation God promised has come.

Through his life, death, and resurrection, Jesus overcomes the brokenness of the world and achieves victory over sin and death. Soon after, he ascends into heaven and, by the power of the Holy Spirit, God's work of transformation in the world continues. Even though Jesus conquered sin, we still live in the wake of its effects on our lives. But, like he has done for all time, God enters into these broken spaces to bring help and healing. As we wait for the return of Christ and the day when sin will be no more, God helps us live with the belief that he is still doing a "new thing." Through his work of transformation in our hearts and lives, God changes our affections and our character to reflect his glory. He gives us comfort, strength, and power, all the while transforming the people and situations around us. In every moment of every day, God is moving us toward his goal of eternal restoration.

Therefore, our present and future hope in God reminds us that there is a *blessing* to be received through his work of transformation in our lives. It reminds us that this work is not new, but one he has been accomplishing since the beginning of time. And, it also reminds us that this transformation is a work that he does both in us and around us.

God Is Doing a New Thing

God is more invested in our spiritual formation than we could ever be. And, sometimes he does his best and brightest work when things are the darkest and most difficult. In fact, he will use what seems like an incredible interruption in our lives to deliver the good things he has promised.[2]

With God, our seasons of longing become a sort of spiritual greenhouse. The weight of our pain is the force through which God grows our trust, faith, and dependency on him. He changes what our hearts love, moving us away from fleeting joys to being grounded in him as the only lasting source of joy. Through his work in our life, we become less controlled by our frustration, anger, or sadness and more controlled by our rootedness in Christ. As we come to realize the limitedness, and often uselessness, of our coping mechanisms, we begin to realize that the hope and fulfillment we desperately desire is only found in Jesus.

The truth is, suffering is not an unusual, surprising experience; it is the experience of everyone who lives in this dramatically broken world.[3] Our lives will always have the companionship of our unwanted friend Longing. So, the hope that God provides us won't do its full work if we don't believe that life with Christ is better than anything else in the world. Ultimately, therefore, *this* is the work of transformation God seeks to do in our life—growing us to believe that above all else, Jesus is better!

Now, I will be the first to say that this has not always *felt* like the good life to me. In my moments of deep sorrow, I have wanted immediate relief. I wanted a life with no pain and Jesus, not *continued pain* and Jesus. But slowly over time, my perspective has changed. Trust me, I would still prefer to have a life with no pain! Yet, I have seen the transformation God has done in me. Through my seasons of longing, he has transformed me into a different person. Specifically, he has transformed the affections of my heart to earnestly desire him more than the things I was using to find immediate but temporary relief.

The "new thing" that God does in us changes how we view and are impacted by our pain. No matter what our situation is, we can be confident that God will not leave us empty-handed nor will he turn his back on us. In our seasons of longing, he changes us. By his grace we become women who are rooted in the truth of his character. Hope for us is the choice to believe that God will not leave us in our pain, but will transform us through it.

In addition to God's internal work of transformation, there are times where he does actually change the circumstances that are causing our longing. When I think about the ways God works miracles in our situations, I am reminded of my friend Autumn. She grew up with a strained relationship with her father. His presence in her life as a child was inconsistent and lacking. By the time I had met her she had a sense of longing that had been tempered by the flakiness of her dad. Autumn longed to have him in her life, but avoided disappointment by having low expectations.

However, after years of no communication between the two of them, the Lord did something powerful. He reconnected Autumn with her dad. Over time he had gotten to a better place emotionally and desired to have a relationship with his daughter. Now, this process of reconnection was not easy because there was a lot of reconciliation that needed to happen. But over several years, even decades, my friend saw God open a door in her life that she had assumed was permanently closed.

The blessing of transformation that God does in our lives, this *new thing* many times results in him changing our situations of longing. He can restore broken relationships, heal our physical bodies, or take away our depression and anxiety. As God reveals himself to us through Scripture, we can't help but see the ways in which his power significantly transformed people's lives. The God of the Bible has not changed, and he is doing that same miraculous work today.

Truth is—some of us will experience God changing the circumstances around us, while others will experience God changing *us* in the midst of circumstances that won't seem to budge. Whether it's our circumstances, our longings, ourselves, or all three, there's one thing all experiences have in common: God is doing a transformative work in some way or another. Because he is a God who transforms. Friend, believe this, and feel the hope that it produces in your soul! God is changing *something* in your life right this very minute. He is a God who is up to the work of restoration, some way, somehow. That's the kind of God he is. That's your hope—no matter how large or looming the giants of Despair and Doubt seem right now.

The Practice of Hope

Knowing that God is up to some sort of transformation in our lives inspires us to continue to pray for change with open hands. Through these prayers we openly express both the desires of our heart and our submission to God's will. For in us, hope cultivates a sense of possibilities without glossing over the realities. It acknowledges life's limitations and incompletions, yet it points toward God.[4] Hope gives us the strength to live in this in-between space as we accept the possibility of change *and* the possibility that our situation might stay the same.

The practice of hope, like our other practices, first calls us to pause and remember the truth of Scripture. Here are a few things the Bible tells us about hope:

- "But those who hope in the LORD will renew their strength. They will soar on wings like eagles; they will run and not grow weary, they will walk and not be faint" (Isa. 40:31 NIV).

- "Behold, the eye of the LORD is on those who fear him, on those who hope in his steadfast love" (Ps. 33:18).

- "I do not cease to give thanks for you, remembering you in my prayers, that the God of our Lord Jesus Christ, the Father of glory, may give you the Spirit of wisdom and of revelation in the knowledge of him, having the eyes of your hearts enlightened, that you may know what is the hope to which he has called you, what are the riches of

his glorious inheritance in the saints"
(Eph. 1:16–18).

- "Let us hold fast the confession of our
  hope without wavering, for he who
  promised is faithful" (Heb. 10:23).
- "May the God of hope fill you with all
  joy and peace in believing, so that by
  the power of the Holy Spirit you may
  abound in hope" (Rom. 15:13).

Even though they are written by different authors, at different times in history and with different versions of pain in the backdrop, they all carry the same message— hope comes from God and is connected to who he surely is and what he is surely doing in the world.

When I think about this work that God is doing, the work he does *while* we are in pain, I think back to Joshua and the nation of Israel. Their new beginning was only received after a long, long time of awaiting a promise. Now, part of their situation did stay the same. God didn't resurrect Moses or erase the grief they experienced because of his death. But if you read through the book of Joshua, you will see that God blessed the nation of Israel immensely and repeatedly. Even though they have story after story of a lot of fighting, God allows Israel to be victorious over and over again. In the midst of their grief, Israel experienced the continual blessing of God in all sorts of ways.

Over the years, it's stories like this one that remind me that even when God doesn't change our immediate situation, he is still at work in our lives. Behind the scenes he is doing work that will bring blessing our way. We just have to have the eyes to see it. Instead of being focused on what we don't have, we have to discipline ourselves to see the overflow of blessing we do have.

Our lives are directly impacted every day through our relationship with God. In his grace, he showers us with both tangible and intangible blessings. It can be as small as a cool breeze on a beautiful day or as big as a new job. Sometimes, he will use others to bless us as well by sending people our way to bless us with encouragement, wisdom, or a small act of kindness.

When the pain of our life is overwhelming, it can be easy to lose focus, believing that God has abandoned us. It is in these very moments that I have learned the power of practicing hope. Here's what it's looked like in my life, and I hope it helps in yours:

1. *Show yourself compassion:* Life is hard and while God shows us grace in our difficulties, many times we do not. The act of showing ourselves compassion reminds us of the love we have received from God. Our journey to find joy will not be perfect, but the One who is perfect loves us perfectly

through it. Our hope is based in the love of Christ and self-compassion helps us remember it.

2. *Show comfort to others:* In the same way that hope gives us love, hope frees us up to love. As we are reminded of what has been given to us, we are able then to use it to bless others. The process of investing in the life of another person who is hurting does something beautiful, both for you and for them.

3. *Celebrate the beauty of God's creation:* hope leads us to believe that what God created is how he describes it—good. Even though sin is a reality of our existence, our understanding of the goodness of life should start in Genesis 1, not Genesis 3. Taking a few moments to recognize the beauty of God's creations helps us remember that he is good and the work of his hands is good. So if he has created beauty in the past, we can hope that he can do it again in the future.

4. *Take a few minutes to review your day to see how God made himself known to you.* Was it through the beauty of his

creation or the kindness of another image-bearer? Was it an answer to a small prayer request or an unusually quiet evening commute home? *All* good things come from God. To remember this, make a daily habit of recording his goodness to you. You'll be surprised how this helps you show up each day with a new perspective!

Hope reminds us that life is a gift. No matter how bad our situation is, God is present with us, working to do a "new thing." He changes our heart affections and shapes our character. Leveraging the weight of our longing, he uses our seasons of pain to develop us to reflect the image of Christ. As I mentioned before, sometimes he will directly change or bring relief for our longing, and other times he will not. But he is always working around us, restoring and transforming and bringing blessings to strengthen and encourage our hearts. He graciously and consistently reminds us that he sees us and that he cares. Hope reminds us that a good life is still possible because we are still connected to the one from whom this goodness flows. It gives us the confidence that despite our longing, we can and will have a life that is blessed, full, and fruitful.

How can you know that, you might wonder? *How can you be sure all this hope and blessing is possible with God?*

Because of God's character, which brings us to the next thing we must stop and embrace in our journey of longing: remembering who God is.

Chapter 5

Embrace Who God Is

I love Chicago. Even though I only lived in the city for a few years, it has always had a special place in my heart. The people, culture, and beautiful chaos has always been exciting to be a part of.

I moved there a few weeks after graduation. My college roommate and I decided to brave a new life in the big city together. We found an apartment in Oak Park, a suburb that bordered right on the west side of Chicago. It was a classic Chicago apartment, with narrow doorways and beautiful crown molding. The windows were huge and gave us a great view of the street below us. We were so excited!

Our excitement grew as our move-in date approached. The day before we were scheduled to move-in, I went to pick up our keys. The apartment manager greeted me and then kindly informed me that we wouldn't be moving in the next day. Whether it had been a miscommunication on their part or the forgetfulness of me and my roommate, our move-in requirements hadn't been met. Specifically, we hadn't fully paid our rental deposit.

While they might tell the story differently, I believe they changed things up on us at the last minute. The rental deposit amount they were now requesting was not the same number they had initially quoted us. In fact, it was an amount my roommate and I didn't have! (I love the city, but do not love how expensive it can be!) Thankfully, the apartment managers gave me and my roommate some time to come up with the extra money. But I left the office that day angry and frustrated! I had been so excited to move in and start my new "after college" life in the city. But because of poor communication, what I had expected to happen, didn't.

Expectations Matter

Our expectations about life determine how we view ourselves, the kind of posture we take toward others, and what decisions we make. For instance, when we expect an interaction with a friend or loved one to be stressful, we might be more reserved or have an unpleasant attitude. On the other hand, when we have expectations that we will be loved unconditionally, we have a willingness to be more transparent.

Most everyone has expectations about pretty much everything. We have expectations about ourselves, our relationships, jobs, and future hopes and dreams. These expectations vary based upon our own life story or the random (and even sometimes judgmental) ideas we can have about a particular person or situation. But, regardless of our difference in expectations, we *all* have expectations about God.

As I've stated before, the greatest enemy of our ability to hope in God is doubt and despair. The fuel for both of these things is often false information. Specifically, this false information usually falls into two categories—lies about God and lies about ourselves. (In this chapter we will cover the first category and we'll walk through the second category in the next chapter.)

When we believe the wrong things about God, we will live wrong. This means that we will internalize toxic information and make poor life decisions based on that information. As we start consuming lies, we begin to believe that God doesn't care about us, he has abandoned us, or worse—our lack of faith is the reason why we have not found relief for our longing. All of these thought clusters serve as an entry door to the black hole of disillusionment, discouragement, and despondency. They welcome us to a path that ends in us checking out on God or being so consumed with our pain that we can't enjoy God or the life he has given us.

Expectations matter, especially our expectations about God.

Learning from Joshua

As we look back to our biblical guide, Joshua, his interaction with God in Joshua 1:3–6 provides some insight into the expectations that we ought to have for God. In these four verses God reaffirms two things: his character and his promises. While calling Joshua to move beyond his pain to embrace his new beginning, God tells Joshua what to expect from him. He says,

> "Every place that the sole of your foot will tread upon I have given to you, just as I promised to Moses. From the wilderness and this Lebanon as far as the great river, the river Euphrates, all the land of the Hittites to the Great Sea toward the going down of the sun shall be your territory. No man shall be able to stand before you all the days of your life. Just as I was with Moses, so I will be with you. I will not leave you or forsake you. Be strong and courageous, for you shall cause this people to inherit the land that I swore to their fathers to give them."

In these verses, God gives Joshua three distinct promises: his *provision*, his *protection,* and his *presence.* But what is notable about these promises is that they are not new. God is repeating promises that he has previously given to Moses and the nation of Israel (and if we trace it back far enough, also to Adam and Eve in Eden!). God's relationship with Israel begins in Genesis but gets renewed in Exodus. After God delivers them out of slavery, he reminds Israel of who he is, who they are, and the relationship he desires to have with them. This is then followed by a ceremony of commitment. Through the giving of the law, specifically the Ten Commandments, God promises that Israel will be his people and that he will be their God (Exod. 6:7).

For the next forty years, Israel journeys with God through the wilderness. During this wandering season, through Moses, God makes many different promises about how he will support and provide for Israel. Right before he dies, Moses reminds Israel of these promises. Here is a bit of what he said:

- "Every place on which the sole of your foot treads shall be yours. Your territory shall be from the wilderness to the Lebanon and from the River, the river Euphrates, to the western sea. No one shall be able to stand against you. The LORD your God will lay the fear of you and the dread of you on all the land that you shall tread, as he promised you" (Deut. 11:24–25).
- "Be strong and courageous. Do not fear or be in dread of them, for it is the LORD your God who goes with you. He will not leave you or forsake you" (Deut. 31:6).
- "It is the LORD who goes before you. He will be with you; he will not leave you or forsake you. Do not fear or be dismayed" (Deut. 31:8).

Joshua would have heard these words. They would have been cemented deep within his heart and mind, especially since they were some of the last words Moses spoke to the people of Israel.

God didn't leave the people wondering what he was like or what to do—he clearly told them what to expect. Said another way, God outlined the proper expectations his people should have about him through promises like the ones above. But let's be honest. Anyone can make a promise. People do it all the time. They talk a big game but then come up short. So on their own, promises can actually be pretty shallow or empty. What makes promises worthwhile is the character of the person making the promise, meaning that the real reason why Joshua could trust in the promises God gave Israel—the real reason he could have proper expectations of God—was because he trusted in the character of God.

Remembering God's Character

The dictionary defines *character* as one of the attributes or features that make up and distinguish an individual.[1] I like to think that character is the essence of a person, a grouping of attributes that help one predict a person's actions or behaviors. Character is what we look to, or should look to, in our attempts to create expectations. If the character of a toddler is mischievous, we expect him to eventually get into very real mischief—and so he does. If we know the character of a politician to be crooked, we expect him to create crooked policies—and without fail, it happens. If we know the character of our neighbor to be kind-hearted, we expect her to wave as we walk past her house—and sure as the sun comes up, so does her hand. And so it is with God. A knowledge of God's character allows us to set appropriate expectations for what he will, and will not, do for us and through us.

When it comes to the character of God, theologians generally create a list of 10–20 traits, including things like *infinite, incomprehensible, omnipresent, omnipotent, omniscient,* and so on. While we could take the rest of the book to focus on all these attributes, we won't.[2] For the purposes of this book, we will highlight three of them: *eternal, sovereign,* and *faithful.*

We all know what it feels like to think God has forgotten us in a season of longing. I distinctly remember the moments I've questioned the validity of God's promises in my life— *Would he really do what he said he would? How can I be sure?* In these moments what grounded me was not my feelings, but the truth of God's character. No matter how often my feelings about a situation change, God's character never does. Learn to trust in what is always true and steady. It will be your anchor when the winds of life are blowing in all directions!

A former seminary professor of mine told me this old saying: "Don't forget in the dark what God told you in the light." We learn about the character of God so that when the lights go out and the longing drags on, we can still see the way forward.

God Is Eternal

When I'm teaching the Bible, I often tell my students that one of the most important tasks of studying Scripture is to ask good questions. One set of questions we should always ask are background questions, for instance, who is the book's author? Who is his original audience and when is he speaking to them? What message was he hoping to convey to them? The answers to these questions help us understand the context in which the book was written.

If we did some research into the background of Genesis, we would learn that the author is Moses and that his audience is the people of Israel. We'd also learn that Israel would have had faint memories of the God of their ancestors,[3] and that Genesis was written to jog their memory, helping them remember the God who had delivered them out of Egypt.

God wanted them to know why he delivered them and how something as horrific as slavery could have become a human institution in the first place. He wanted them to know his character, so they would have appropriate expectations, both for what he would do for them and require of them.

Genesis opens with the words, "In the beginning God created the heavens and the earth." In one verse God tells us something foundational about himself: he existed before creation. There is also another important truth that I'll just throw in here for free—God also lets them know there is only one God! Having either worshiped or simply been exposed to the false gods of Egypt, Israel might have been confused about who was in control of the world. With these ten words, God clears up that confusion for them—he alone was in control.

The statement of existence in Genesis 1:1 points to God's eternality. This one verse lets Israel, and us, know that God was not created but existed before creation. *But how does this truth affect my real life,* you may ask? I think Jen Wilkin gets it right when she says, "Free to act within time as he wills, he exists outside of it. He is simultaneously the God of the past, present, and future, bending time to his perfect will, unfettered by its constraints. The past holds for him not a missed opportunity. The present holds for him no anxiety. The future holds for him no uncertainty . . . moreover, all of God's actions within time happen at just the right time."[4]

Our ability to trust in the promises of God, and therefore have proper expectations of him, can be hindered by the way we are consumed with time. The thoughts we have about the past, present, and future can control us in ways that are unhealthy and ungodly. Sometimes we just love to replay in our minds the tape of our past wounds and disappointments over and over again. Others of us have an over-fascination with the future that leaves us in a perpetual state of anxiety. This type of mental escapism also hinders us from appropriately showing up in the present.

The lies of doubt and despair can lead us to trust in our own timing rather than the timing of God. When the provision doesn't come when we desire it, we can begin to question whether it will come at all. But in the moments I am tempted to believe these lies myself, I remember the words of a gospel song I sang as a kid—the one that reminded me that though he might not show up when I wanted him, he'll always be there "right on time" because he's an "on time God. Yes He is."

God's eternality means that his timing is always perfect. So, when we trust in this attribute of his character, we make good use of our time as we wait for him to fulfill his promises.[5] We don't overly focus on the past or the future, but we live in the present, focused on the work he is currently doing in our lives.

Friend, are your thoughts consumed about what happened in the past? Are you losing sleep worrying about what's coming up ahead? Do you feel like God is about to miss his small window of opportunity to give you what you long for? Remember that God has not forgotten about you. Remember that he will keep his promises and is working for your good. Fight to trust that his timing is perfect! He *will* come through for you.

God Is Sovereign

Another key attribute that influences our ability to trust in God's promises is his sovereignty. When I think about the sovereignty of God, I am reminded of the words of A. W. Pink: "Subject to none, influenced by none, absolutely independent; God does as He pleases, only as He pleases, always as He pleases."[6] In my Elizabeth translation, "God does what he wants to when he wants to because he can!"

We find the first announcement of God's sovereignty in the same place we learn about his eternality, Genesis 1:1. By declaring himself to be the author of all creation, God sets himself apart from creation. As the creator of all things, he alone gets to decide how his world and his creation should function. He alone is in control. But because he is in control, he can work all things for our good, even those things that others mean for our evil.[7]

If we were to rewind the tape of Israel's story a bit, we would read about a man named Joseph. Familiar to many of us, Joseph had a few brothers who didn't like him. Their disdain for him was so great that they actually sold him into slavery. (I feel pretty comfortable classifying their actions as evil.) But, even though they did not intend good things for their brother, God had other plans for Joseph's life.

In Genesis 37–50, we are given the details of Joseph and his family. After being sold into slavery and changing hands a couple times, Joseph is bought by an Egyptian officer. And in that officer's house, Joseph's fate seems to get worse as he endures a false rape allegation. Then things get even more terrible as he faces an undeserved stint in prison. In prison, he shows himself useful, and it seems as if all his hard work might help him get released—yet time and time again, his longing for freedom goes forgotten and unmet. Eventually, however, he helps the Pharaoh to such a level that the king not only releases him but makes him second in command over all of Egypt! In over thirteen years, Joseph goes from being a slave to governing over those who bought him as a slave. But that's not all. He also ends up governing over those very brothers who sold him into slavery.

Do you remember how it happened? Now in his position of prominence, long after they sold him into slavery, Joseph's brothers come to Egypt. Why? Because their land was facing a famine and Egypt had food. They didn't know it, but God had raised up Joseph to help lead during this season. So, imagine their surprise when the brothers figured out the identity of the person they had to come get help from—Joseph!

In a beautiful story of forgiveness, Joseph ends up offering his entire family protection and provision under his care. He had the power to take vengeance against his brothers, but he chose to extend them grace.

At the end of the story, in Genesis 50, we read about the death of Joseph's father. With the passing of the family patriarch, Joseph's brothers get concerned. They think Joseph's grace to them was only because of their father. With him now gone, Joseph had the power to do them great harm. But instead of acting in vengeance toward them, this is what he says: "As for you, you meant evil against me, but God meant it for good, to bring it about that many people should be kept alive, as they are today" (Gen. 50:20). In his sovereignty, God had taken their evil deeds and reworked them to bring good to thousands and thousands of people.

In our seasons of longing, we can easily question the work of God in our lives. Situations of prolonged suffering or disappointment make it difficult to see any possibility for good coming out of our pain. But when we trust in the sovereignty of God, we trust that he is in full control of everything. We also trust that his ways are best, and that he can take any hard thing and use it for good.

Now, this is not always an easy truth to believe. Some of the things we experience in this life are hard and traumatic. But in spite of it all, God is in control and he truly is working things out for our good. Again, sometimes God does his best and brightest work when things are the darkest and most difficult.[8] He is not off to the side, unconcerned about what is happening in our lives. He is actively involved in us living with and overcoming our places of pain and discomfort.

So our first response to God's sovereignty should be to trust that he is at work and that he knows what he is doing. Sometimes we can confuse the middle of our story for the end of our story. Just because it isn't clear to us doesn't mean it isn't clear to God. He's got everything under control.

Our second response to God's sovereignty is obedience. As we walk in step with him, he will lead us to do certain things. This could be as simple as patiently waiting for him to answer a prayer request or as risky as us taking a step of faith. Many times, the wisdom or discernment God will give us will not always make sense to our logical brains. Over the years I've come to realize that God does not give me all the information: he just gives me the information I need. As we search his Word, listen to him in prayer, and lean into the counsel of trusted community, our responsibility is to obey the directions he gives us —even when we don't fully understand.

Friend, are you angry with God? Do you question why he allowed you to experience the things you have gone through or the situations you are living in? Do you feel overwhelmed because it seems as if your life is spinning out of control? Remember that he is not unaware or caught off guard by your situation; God is in control, which means he has a plan and a purpose for your longing. Fight to trust and find rest in his sovereignty, being obedient to the direction he gives you, even if it is to simply be still (Ps. 46:10).

God Is Faithful

Alongside God being both eternal and sovereign, another thing to remember in seasons of longing is that God is also faithful. When we question whether or not God will even show up in our lives, our submission to his faithfulness helps us remember that he always keeps his promises. Our God is faithful in all things, at all times.[9] Faithfulness is the cornerstone of trustworthiness; it is the act of being reliable, steadfast, and unwavering.[10] The fuel for our expectations, inherent within the essence of faithfulness, is an assurance of dependency. Unlike man, God will not let us down. So, for God to be faithful means that we can trust he will fulfill whatever promises he makes. Whatever he says *will* come to pass.

Joshua and Israel would have known that God was, "the faithful God who keeps covenant and steadfast love with those who love him and keep his commandments, to a thousand generations" (Deut. 7:9). After being delivered out of Egypt, God made a commitment to Israel. He agreed to be their God (Exod. 6:7), uniting himself to them through covenant. Now, God's covenantal agreement with Israel had some stipulations. If they obeyed his laws, he would bless them; if they were disobedient, he would curse them. But, either way, God promised to be eternally faithful to Israel. During their forty years in the wilderness this faithfulness would manifest itself through provision of food and victory in battle. But the ultimate example of God's faithfulness was Israel's second chance crossing of the Jordan River that we read about in Joshua 1.

You see, after delivering Israel out of Egypt, God had given Israel a chance to take ownership of the land he had promised them through their forefather Abraham (Gen. 12:1–7). Remember how, after sending a few spies to scout out the land, the people decided against taking the gift that God had promised them? Remember how the land was occupied by other people and the Israelites were afraid? Out of fear they rejected God's blessing. Yet, every declaration God has made he will fulfill, for "God is not man, that he should lie, or a son of man, that he should change his mind. Has he said, and will he not do it? Or has he spoken, and will he not fulfill it?" (Num. 23:19). This means that what God promised Abraham was going to be accomplished, even if it wasn't with this specific generation of Israelites.

If we look back to the story, we see that after Israel rejected God's blessing of the land, they ended up wandering for forty years in the wilderness. They experienced forty years of setting up and tearing down campsites. They fought numerous battles and had several heated arguments with God. They walked, and walked, and walked as they waited for God to bless them.

Fast-forward to God's conversation with Joshua—now very familiar to you—in Joshua 1:2: "Moses my servant is dead. Now therefore arise, go over this Jordan, you and all this people, *into the land that I am giving to them, to the people of Israel*" (emphasis added). Do you see what's happening here? What Joshua is about to lead the people into is not some random, new future that has no connection to the seasons behind them. Rather, Joshua is about to lead them into the fulfillment of God's promise to Abraham. God didn't scrap his plans. He shows up to this new generation, the same promise and future in hand, as he did to the generations before. "Go into the land I am giving them." As Joshua heard these words, he would have been clearly reminded of the faithfulness of God. What might have seemed like an unnecessary detour or evidence of a forgetful God was the opposite. God never forgot his promise and now, forty years later, he was making good on the words he had said.

In our seasons of longing, it can be very easy to think that God has forgotten us. When suffering continues, uninterrupted, for extended periods of time, it can be easy to feel that God does not care or that he will not make good on his promises. The faithfulness of God reminds us that while these feelings are real, they are also untrue. God does not abandon his people. He always makes good on his promises. So, as we fight to see the work God is doing in our lives, we need to remember that he is always faithful. He will show up, right on time, with exactly what we need.

Remembering God's Promises

During my time serving in church ministry, I would always try to recruit new volunteers. Every year, some volunteers would leave for one reason or another. Anticipating this transition, I liked to have a regular inflow of new volunteers into our ministry. As a church leader, you learn to observe the character of people who regularly attend the church. Do they show up consistently? Do they participate in ministry programs? Are they willing to serve with small tasks when asked? These and a few other criteria were on my mental "potential volunteer" checklist.

I ran through these questions in my mind when I met Tasha. She had regularly attended some ministry programs I oversaw, so I thought she might be interested in serving as a volunteer. As I began to task Tasha with responsibilities, I saw that she was a go-getter. Both my personal interactions with her and her recommendations showed me that she was dependable. If I gave her a task, I could expect her to get it done. Or, if she told me she needed a bit of creative freedom with an idea, I knew that what she would create would turn out to be awesome! Based upon her character, I had a clear understanding of what I could expect from her.

As I've touched on before, character is the filter through which we are able to create expectations. When we know that someone is dependable or the opposite—undependable—we are able to create certain expectations for their behavior. If this is true for us as humans, *how much more do you think this is true for God?*

Knowing God's character helps us have appropriate expectations for how he will show up in our lives. It helps us know what he has, and has not, promised us. The consistency of his character gives us the ability to trust in him. Regardless of how we may feel, God's character shows us that his promises are true and will be fulfilled.

The promises of God serve as a powerful lifeline during seasons of longing. They are unwavering truths that we can root ourselves in, providing us with a much-needed sense of stability and strength. By way of reminder, in Joshua 1:3–6, God promises Joshua three things: *provision, protection,* and *presence.* Even though these promises cover different needs Joshua would have, what God is really promising in these verses is himself. God is promising that the fullness of his character and power would go with Joshua into his next season. For this reason, I believe what God promised Joshua are promises that you and I can trust in as well. Our faith in Jesus unites us into a relationship with God. Because of Christ we get access to the fullness of God's character and power. So the same provision, protection, and presence that God offers Joshua, he offers to us too!

God's Provision

God gives his first promise to Joshua in Joshua 1:3–4. He says, "Every place that the sole of your foot will tread upon I have given to you, just as I promised to Moses. From the wilderness and this Lebanon as far as the great river, the river Euphrates, all the land of the Hittites to the Great Sea toward the going down of the sun shall be your territory." The geographic boundaries that God lists off would have been the general boundaries of the land of Canaan. A repetition of Genesis 12:1–7 and Deuteronomy 11:24, God was promising Joshua the provision of physical land. But this land was not a random gift. God was giving Israel what they needed to accomplish the task he gave them. Remember the plan of redemption that we talked about in the last chapter? Abraham and Israel are a huge part of that.

In Genesis 12, God singles out Abraham to be the man, and eventually the nation, through which he will work his plan of redemption in the world. He tells Abraham that he will bless him and his family, but that they will be used by God to be a blessing to the entire world! As part of this "blessing package," God promises to give Abraham and his descendants the land of Canaan.

You might be asking yourself—of all things that God could promise Abraham, why land?

Well, for Israel, land meant influence. If you were to pull out a map, you would see that Canaan is a connecting point between Asia Minor, Asia, and Africa. Extending across the major trade route between these countries, the land of Canaan was ideally situated to serve as a focal point for cultural exchange. It was God's intention that Canaan would serve as the staging area for the proclamation of the truth about God to the nations that didn't believe in him.[11] The land of Canaan was given to Israel so that they could physically be around the very people God wanted them to reach. God's provision was intended to help them fulfill *his* redemptive purposes.

Similarly, through the person and work of Christ, you and I have been called by God to be a part of his redemptive work in the world. While it might seem like an interruption or a detour, our seasons of longing are as much a part of this work as any other season in our lives. The entirety of our lives is to be lived to glorify God and to further his work in the world. This means that God is invested in supplying us with everything we *need* not only to survive but to thrive!

His provision is both tangible and intangible. I believe God provides for our physical needs—money to pay bills, healing for our body and minds, a new supportive friendship, or the right school for a child with special needs. He also provides for the intangibles, giving us *his* wisdom, peace, comfort, love, and strength. But don't take my word for it! Here is a bit of what the Scriptures say God promises to provide us with:

- Physical needs (Matt. 6:31–33)
- Peace (Phil. 4:6–7)

- Grace (2 Cor. 9:8–11)
- Strength (2 Cor. 12:9–10)
- Wisdom (James 1:5)
- Comfort (2 Cor. 1:3)
- *All we need* (Phil. 4:19)

I remember the nights when the clouds of depression were swirling above me and my pillow was soaked with tears. My heart was heavy with sorrow, and I was questioning whether or not God even cared. In those moments of despair and doubt, I have been met by the faithful provision of God. Sometimes it has been an unexpected call or text from a friend, saying that they are praying for me. I've had surprise gifts show up at my door, unexpected checks show up in my mailbox, and situations where I could literally feel the peace of God calming my soul.

Most of all, I have seen this same God recalibrate my heart and mind. He has continually used his Word to remind me that my life is bigger than the gap of longing I may feel. He has reassured me of his work in my life and given me eyes to see the joy he is bringing my way.

We serve a God who will give us what we need when we need it! His goal is to help us live the life he has given us, so we can accomplish the purpose he has set out for us. If you are struggling today, friend, take heart in this: God promises to be your provider. He made good on this promise to Joshua, and he will make good on it to you.

God's Protection

God's second promise comes to Joshua in Joshua 1:5a, "No man shall be able to stand before you all the days of your life." With a few words, God promises Joshua protection, specifically against anyone who would seek to come up against Joshua and do him harm.

The land God gave Israel was a wonderful blessing. But it came with one important piece of information—it was not vacant. Canaan was inhabited by other nations, nations that Israel would spend a considerable amount of time fighting after they crossed over the Jordan River. Here is a quick peek into who Israel would have to fight in order to take control of the land that God had given them:

- Jericho (Josh. 7:2–6)
- Ai and Bethel (8:1–29)
- The Amorites (10:1–27)
- Makkedah (10:28)
- Libnah (10:29–30)
- Lachish (10:31–32)
- Gezer (10:33)
- Eglon (10:34–35)
- Hebron (10:36–37)
- Debir (10:38–39)
- Northern Cities (11:1–9)
- Hazor (11:12–17)

In all, Joshua and Israel fought and won against thirty-one different kings in the land of Canaan. That's a lot of fighting!

But in all these battles, Israel only lost once, and that was because of disobedience to God. In every other battle they won.

In his sovereignty, God allowed Israel to engage a significant amount of difficulty as they sought to take control of the land he had given them. Some of the opposition Israel faced was small; some of it was big. But in every situation God gave them the victory. As we read through the entirety of Israel's story, their consistent victory in battle is a repeated theme. Israel will seek God before battle, he will give them his blessing, and then they will go win the battle. This happens over and over and over again. Nothing, and no one, was going to thwart the specific plan that God had for Israel!

Each time I reread the story of Israel, there is one detail that always stands out to me—what God *doesn't* promise them. He doesn't promise Joshua that Israel will have a journey devoid of difficulty. He never promises that they won't have to fight against enemies or overcome any obstacles. What he promised was that in the midst of all those things, he would protect them. And, God's protection would lead to their continual victory.

Hardship, trouble, and struggle, can seem like common companions in a season of longing or suffering. Whether the obstacles are internal or external, we can easily become overwhelmed and discouraged. The weight of the pain becomes too much and it seems like we only have two options—give in or give up. But the story of Joshua shows that we have a third option—we can fight back.

You and I live in a fallen world and are in a constant battle against sin, our flesh, the world, and the enemy. So not only should we expect opposition; we should expect that the opposition will be both physical and spiritual.

Physical opposition comes in all shapes and sizes. Sometimes it is an actual person or group of people in our lives who are actively seeking to do us harm or disrupt our lives. It can be a frustrating situation, where we keep experiencing closed doors. Or, sometimes it's the mental strain of our season of longing. As each day becomes increasingly difficult, simple tasks become overwhelming. With each passing moment it feels as if life is beating us down.

On the other hand, spiritual opposition can be just as varied and weighty. In Ephesians 6:10–20, Paul warns us about the powers and principalities we battle against. He tells us to "put on the whole armor of God, that you may be able to stand against the schemes of the devil." In this passage, Paul's words are sober but hopeful. He acknowledges the spiritual realities we live in, but also reminds us about the spiritual power we have been given because of our redemption through Christ.

Whether our struggles are physical or spiritual, God offers those of us in Christ protection. The protection God offered Joshua was connected to the purpose he had for his life and for Israel. God was invested in making sure that Israel reached their goal. In the same way, God is invested in making sure that we reach the purpose he has set out for us. For this reason, God gives us the strength and means to fight. But he also goes before us to fight on our behalf.

We serve a God who is aware of the struggles we are carrying and going through. He is not on the sidelines unconcerned or oblivious to our pain. He sees it and works to show up in it. Now, the substance and timing of God's protection in our lives might not be what we want it to be. But trust—in our greatest moments of difficulty, God is fighting for us.

God's Presence

God gives his third promise in Joshua 1:5b. He says, "Just as I was with Moses, so I will be with you. I will not leave you or forsake you." However, as we have seen before, it is a promise that is not new.

God's promise of presence is a repetition of the promise he gave to Joshua in Deuteronomy 31:23 and, through Moses, in Deuteronomy 31:8. He also gave the same promise to Moses in Exodus 3:12, Jacob in Genesis 31:3, and Isaac in Genesis 26:3. In the same way that God had promised to be present with Joshua's forefathers, he was going to be present with him. This consistency is evidence both of God's faithfulness and the continuity of his purpose. He had been unwavering in his goal to bless Abraham's descendants and to use them to bless the world. Now, with Joshua representing a new generation of Israelites, God is promising to continue a commitment he began long before.

But there is one more verse in Scripture that is a repetition of God's words to Joshua. It is Matthew 28:19–20. Through the person and work of Jesus, God makes the same commitment of presence to you and me. No matter how hard a situation gets or how many sinful decisions we may make, God will never leave us. Not only will he be present by our side for eternity, but by the power of the Holy Spirit, he is always with us because he is *in* us. We can't get away from God's presence if we tried!

Let's be honest though, many of us are aware that God is present with us on a daily basis. And, if we were being *really* honest, we might also share how his presence did not prevent us from experiencing longing or suffering. So, even though God is present with us all the time, *why does it matter?*

This is a question we usually ask when we have the option of choosing to find comfort in God's presence or comfort in something else. Sometimes, the idea of the indwelling presence of God in our lives can seem really intangible and/or a bit ethereal. We can be quick to minimize or misunderstand it simply because we can't actually *see* God. Out of sight, out of mind.

While it may be hard to understand, God's presence in our lives is not passive. He's not like one of our old roommates, keeping us company as we watch our favorite TV show. On the contrary, to dwell with the creator of the universe is a nearness that comes with access to the fullness of his character. He does not just show up and stand still, he shows up and acts on our behalf.

When we feel as if we lack the resources to deal with what we are facing, the promise of God's presence reminds us that we have more potential than we could have on our own.[12] His comfort holds us close when it seems as if nothing can take away the pain we are feeling. When no one understands, he does. When we feel forgotten, misunderstood, and rejected, he sees, knows, and loves us deeply.

Ultimately, to have God's presence with us means that we access the fullness of his character. In other words, with his here-forever presence, comes his here-forever wisdom, his here-forever grace, his here-forever strength, his here-forever authority, his here-forever love, his here-forever mercy, his here-forever righteousness, and his here-forever patience. God's presence guarantees that in your suffering you will have everything you need.[13] The depth by which our hearts can be impacted by God's presence is unmatched, for no created thing can heal and transform our lives better than the Creator.

We serve a God who is not far off, but who is near. In every difficulty we face, he is right by our side working on our behalf. But if this promise sounds a bit similar to the other two, it is. God's provision and his protection show up in our lives *because* God is present with us and *within* us. Through the work of Christ and by the power of the Holy Spirit, God's presence is the access door to all the promises he has given us throughout Scripture. It is only because he is with us that he provides for our needs, protects us from danger, and does an overall work of transformation in our lives.

As I think back to my experience recruiting ministry volunteers, I remember another volunteer I recruited at the same time I recruited Tasha. She had been a regular attendee and was full of lots of energy. Taking a risk, I ended up adding her to the team. From my conversations with her I expected that she would do great! I was wrong.

Looking back, I had made a quick decision. Some of the bumps we hit could have been avoided by getting a bit more information about her ministry experience and maybe a few recommendations. I would have placed her on a different team, and she would have been wonderful! But because I didn't have good information, I had the wrong expectations. And, in hindsight, those expectations led me to make some poor decisions that affected her and the ministry.

Expectations matter, especially our expectations about God. Bad theology about the character of God can lead us to make poor decisions. We can think God is holding out on us, when he is offering us blessing. We can think God is punishing us, when he is offering us his grace. We can think God has forgotten us, when he is present with us, offering us the fullness of himself. No matter what happens, we serve a God who is always with us, and it's in his character and promises that we ground our hope. So when the longing goes on longer than you'd like and the road seems hard, *remember*. Remember who he is. Remember he is eternal—he is not getting the timing wrong! Remember he is sovereign—even the worst parts of the journey cannot escape his hand as he turns them for good! Remember he is faithful—he will always deliver on his promises to take care of you, protect you, and go with you!

The Practice of Remembrance || God's Character and Promises

Here's the thing about remembering who God is— it's hard to remember what you don't actually know. By his grace, the Holy Spirit is able to bring truth to our minds, but this doesn't mean we have no part to play. On the contrary, we cooperate with God's Spirit by filling our minds with God's Word. Throughout Scripture we see constant reminders for the people of God to be proactive about remembering the truth about who God is. For Israel many of these reminders pointed them to rehearse the story of their deliverance from Egypt.

- "And it shall be to you as a sign on your hand and as a memorial between your eyes, that the law of the LORD may be in your mouth. For with a strong hand the LORD has brought you out of Egypt" (Exod. 13:9).

- "You shall remember that you were a slave in the land of Egypt, and the LORD your God brought you out from there with a mighty hand and an outstretched arm. Therefore the LORD your God commanded you to keep the Sabbath day" (Deut. 5:15).

- "But it is because the LORD loves you and is keeping the oath that he swore to your fathers, that the LORD has brought you out with a mighty hand and redeemed you from the house of slavery, from the hand of Pharaoh king of Egypt. Know therefore that the

LORD your God is God, the faithful
God who keeps covenant and steadfast
love with those who love him and keep
his commandments, to a thousand
generations" (Deut. 7:8–9).

- "Then the people answered, 'Far be
it from us that we should forsake the
LORD to serve other gods, for it is
the LORD our God who brought us
and our fathers up from the land of
Egypt, out of the house of slavery,
and who did those great signs in our
sight and preserved us in all the way
that we went, and among all the peo-
ples through whom we passed'" (Josh.
24:16–17).

As Israel retold the story of their deliverance, they
were reminded of the character of their God. In particular, they were reminded about how the past actions
of God would repeat themselves in their present and
future. And then, over time, those stories got recorded in
Scripture for all of us to look back on and remember. So,
the best way for us to remember the character and promises of God is for us to look for him in the place where
he reveals himself to us the most—the Bible. Here are
three quick questions you ask *every time* you are reading
through a verse or passage:

1. *What does this verse/passage teach me about God?*

   The Bible is a book about God; every verse or passage we read tells us about him. As you are reading, learn to identify the attribute of God the passage highlights. If you aren't familiar with God's attributes, here is a short list to get you started:

   Holy, just, faithful, wise, righteous, gracious, eternal, love, merciful, sovereign, omnipotent, omnipresent, immutable, transcendent, immanent.[14]

2. *What promise is God making in this passage?*

   The promises of God are connected to his character. So as you read through Scripture, look for promises that are true for all believers. Again, here is a quick list to get you started:

   Comfort, wisdom, peace, hope, joy, a renewed heart and mind, protection, grace, forgiveness, eternal life.

3. *How can I respond to this truth today?*

   As we've talked about in this chapter, the truth of God's character and promises helps us to see our situation and longing with new eyes. But it also gives us hope to hold onto throughout each moment of the day. So, after you identify the attribute or promise a particular passage highlights, take a few moments to think through how you can actively trust in, exemplify, and honor that attribute. Here are a few examples:

Lord, because you are faithful, I will trust that you have not forgotten me and will be faithful to keep your promises.

Lord, your love reminds me that I am valuable simply because I am yours. Help me find my value in your love and not the love of others.

Lord, your grace reminds me that you give your children blessings, even when we don't deserve them. Help me see and rejoice over the blessings you will bring my way today.

The Bible helps us learn what we can expect God to be for us, no matter the situation. So expect him to stay true to his character. Expect him to stay true to *you*.

Speaking of *you*, now that we've taken a good look at God, let's consider the next thing we can embrace in our journey of longing.

Chapter 6

Embrace Who You Are

I met Nikki at church. A funny, energetic, and dramatic woman, Nikki is an actress. But in her mid-twenties, her acting career was cut short as a chronic disease began to ravage her body. Over a decade later, Nikki is still fighting to live, having some good days and lots of hard ones. Instead of being on a movie set or a theatre stage, she is going to doctor's appointments and managing a bunch of different medications. She makes time to work on podcasts, acting classes, and other creative projects as she can. But everything she does is at the mercy of her health.

Every so often Nikki and I get together to catch up on life. The last time we got together, we talked about all the usual things—updates on mutual friends, the TV shows we had been watching, and how we both were going to put work into meeting that special someone in the next few months. But then she told me some tragic news—a few months earlier one of her family members had died. In his early thirties, his life had suddenly been taken from him.

As she was talking to me about the pain of her grief, she talked about how his death had given her a new perspective about life. She said, "I have to live because he can't." Even though her health was not getting better, I could hear a renewed vibrancy in her desire to fight to live. Nikki talked about getting a new doctor, trying to find new health treatments, and the power of having a fighting mindset. She spoke of the future with hope. Now, Nikki wasn't naively optimistic, but rather believed that the life that remained in her body was a blessing from God to be stewarded with the fullness of her being.

When we are fueled by a fresh sense of possibilities, hope provides us with a new perspective. It reminds us that with God there is always a new beginning. In the midst of despair-filled circumstances, it is imperative to hear God saying, "In every end lies a new beginning—can you see yours?" Hope reminds us that if there is still breath in our bodies, there is still life for us to live. And taking hold of that hope, as we've discussed in the last chapter, comes through not only believing who God is as he's revealed himself to be in his Word, but remembering who God is when our circumstances tempt us to forget or question his character. On top of that, or rather in light of it, hope also comes by remembering who we are.

We Have Forgotten Who We Are

Seasons of longing can be overwhelming because they become all-consuming. If we are not careful, we will dedicate a considerable amount of time to thinking or talking about the object of our longing. All of our decisions will be made with it in mind. So much so, that our lives become defined not by God, but by what our heart desperately desires.

Tragically, what usually gets lost in this process is our sense of purpose. As humans, most of us have probably asked the question "What am I supposed to do with my life?" While finding one's destiny is the topic of many recent books on the New York Times Best Sellers List, it isn't a new conversation, nor one that is foreign to the Bible. In fact, the Bible provides an answer to this question in its first chapter, as God gives humanity their divine identity and calling in Genesis 1 (more on that is coming up in a moment!). But, somehow along the way, as we become stuck in our seasons of longing, we forget these words and, in some sense, forget the truth about who God says we are and what he has called us to do.

Learning from Joshua

In Joshua 1:6–9, the focus of God's words to Joshua changes. He transitions from talking about himself, to talking about Joshua. After reminding Joshua of his character and his promises, God proceeds to give him a few instructions. He tells him,

"Be strong and courageous, for you shall cause this people to inherit the land that I swore to their fathers to give them. Only be strong and very courageous, being careful to do according to all the law that Moses my servant commanded you. Do not turn from it to the right hand or to the left, that you may have good success wherever you go. This Book of the Law shall not depart from your mouth, but you shall meditate on it day and night, so that you may be careful to do according to all that is written in it. For then you will make your way prosperous, and then you will have good success. Have I not commanded you? Be strong and courageous. Do not be frightened, and do not be dismayed, for the LORD your God is with you wherever you go."

In his faithfulness, what God had promised almost 700 years earlier to Abraham was now being fulfilled. Through Joshua's leadership, Israel would take hold of the promised land of Canaan.

Want to know something that always stands out to me in this story? It's how Joshua's purpose was connected to a story that was bigger than his own life or the life of the people he was leading. God had been working through Israel to bless the entire world. This would have been a story that Joshua and Israel were well acquainted with. In fact, they would repeat it to one another regularly through the reading of the Book of the Law at religious festivals and worship ceremonies.

What comes to mind when you hear "the Book of the Law" mentioned in Scripture? Perhaps the Ten Commandments? Maybe Exodus? Those are true to an extent, but incomplete. As it turns out, the Book of the Law is the first five books of the Bible, written by Moses—Genesis, Exodus, Leviticus, Numbers, and Deuteronomy. Starting in Genesis, the Book of the Law would explain God's creation of the world, his concern for it, the covenant he made with Israel, the stories of how he had freed them from oppression in the past, the promises he had in store for them in the future, and the ways he expected them to live in the "here and now." As God's people heard each of these books, they would retell their own history, emphasizing their religious, cultural, and moral heritage. They would also be reminded of their future destiny.[1] Every time it was read, either in part or whole, the Book of the Law reminded Israel about their identity and purpose.

God tells Joshua that his success is directly related to whether or not he obeys all that is written in the Book of the Law. Now when we hear this, we might think God is telling Joshua that he needs to perfectly keep a list of rules. And we would be *kinda* right. Israel had agreed to live in a certain way, knowing that obedience to God's commands would bring blessing their way. Likewise, disobedience would bring negative consequences. Yet, when God tells Joshua to "be careful to do according to all that is written in it," he is not promoting legalism but ultimately reminding him of something deeper.

By following the words in the Book of the Law, Joshua would be living in light of his divine identity and purpose.

Identity

Superhero movies are my jam. Whether it's *X-Men, The Avengers, Wonder Woman,* or *Batman,* I find lots of enjoyment watching people with superpower try to save the world. One of my favorite superhero movies is *Black Panther.* If you haven't seen it, I need you to put this book down, go watch it, and then come back! Seriously though, if you have not seen it you definitely need to watch it. You will not be disappointed.

Like most superhero movies, this movie is the story of the title character—Black Panther. The movie takes place in Wakanda, Africa, where the Black Panther rules as King T'Challa. (Just in case you were wondering, Wakanda is not an actual country in Africa.) There is one scene toward the beginning of the movie where T'Challa's father, the king, has just died and now T'Challa is being crowned king. During this ceremony another leader named M'Baku challenges him for his throne. This challenge leads to a ceremonial fight between the two in front of the royal family and other royal leaders. At a certain point, the fight gets bad—really bad. Taking blow after blow, T'Challa is losing, and in one of his weakest moments of seeming failure, his mother yells out, "Tell them who you are!" As he hears these words, his demeanor changes. Once bowed down in weakness and defeat, he starts to rise with renewed fervor. T'Challa then raises his head high, and in epic fashion, he yells out: "I am Prince T'Challa, son of

King T'Chaka!" By declaring his identity, T'Challa gains the strength he needs to win the fight.

Every time I watch this scene I tear up. To watch him gain so much power and internal strength from the declaration of his identity is overwhelming in all the best ways. But I also tear up because of how this story reminds me of what we, as Christians, are able to do when we remember who we are and whose we are.

Like Joshua, our story begins with Genesis 1. After describing how God created the world, Moses tells the story of how God created humanity. In Genesis 1:26–28 he writes,

> God said, "Let us make man in our image, after our likeness. And let them have domin-ion over the fish of the sea and over the birds of the heavens and over the livestock and over all the earth and over every creeping thing that creeps on the earth." So God created man in his own image, in the image of God he created him; male and female he created them. And God blessed them. And God said to them, "Be fruitful and multiply and fill the earth and subdue it, and have dominion over the fish of the sea and over the birds of the heavens and over every living thing that moves on the earth."

There are two foundational truths that Moses unveils for us in these verses. One, we are made in the image of God.

Two, our divine purpose is connected to caring for the world God created.

At my home church, I have the privilege of teaching people how to study the Bible. During my introductory session, I usually frame our reading of the Bible along the same lines as eavesdropping on a conversation. (Go with me here. I promise this makes sense!) While the Bible was written for our benefit, it was not actually written directly to us at first. It was written originally to some other audience in some other time period, which means that oftentimes, there will be certain words or phrases that carry a lot of significance to that audience but make no sense to us at first glance. Why? Because those same words or phrases are not used in our modern-day vernacular! The word *image* falls into this category.

The Bible was written in a culture of kings and kingdoms. In Israel's day, kings would have sculptures of themselves created, and then they'd leave those statues, or images, in the places they ruled so people would remember who the king was when he was not physically present. These statues were built according to the king's likeness on purpose, so both citizens and travelers could easily identify and remember whose land they were in. And these "images" would weigh tons and could be 20–30 feet high! Why so large, you might wonder? To remind the people of one thing—the majesty and glory of the king. So, when Moses uses the word *image* to refer to our divine identity, he is letting us know that humanity was created to represent the majesty and glory of God to the world.

You and I were created to show the world what God is like. When people interact with us, they should see God's character, his goodness, justice, mercy, righteousness, kindness, holiness, and so much more. People should know what God is like by interacting with us. We were created to bring glory to God. However, this divine identity carries another important truth—because we are made in God's image not as lifeless statues but as living beings, every human is valuable and has inherent dignity and worth.

Vulnerability and decreased capacity often accompany prolonged seasons of suffering. In the words of my sister, "we walk with a limp." Many times this "limp" is apparent to other people or hinders our ability to interact with those around us. With certain groups of people, we constantly feel different or out of place. This can cause us to internalize feelings of unworthiness, believing that what we lack makes us undeserving of acceptance or blessing.

I know singles who have been excluded from community with their married counterparts or service opportunities within the church because of their lack of a spouse. I also know people who have disabilities or chronic illnesses who have endured hurtful assumptions that they have nothing of significance to give to others. When we don't measure up to artificial societal standards of beauty, success, intelligence, or what people consider "normal," we can begin to entertain unbiblical thoughts about our identity.

By viewing ourselves through the lens of our longing instead of God's Word, we grow to see our identity through the lens of what we lack rather than as an image-bearer. In these moments, we need to follow in the way of Joshua, remembering the words of the Book of the Law. As we recite the truth of Genesis 1:26–28 to ourselves, we are reminded of our true identity.

Our life has value because of the one who gave us life. Where longing would strip us of our identity and convince us that we are missing out on a better life, the truth in Genesis 1 tells us something different. It reminds us our best life is in reflecting the character of God to the people around us. Whether it's in a hospital room or our living room, giving glory to God is something we all can do. *Each and every one of us can remind the world of what God is like.* There is no greater identity than to be an image-bearer and child of the Most High God!

Calling

Every so often a video will come across my social media feed that I end up sharing with all my friends. Sometimes it's really funny and sometimes it's deeply inspirational. Sometimes it's both, and let's be honest, sometimes it's just an opportunity for me to distract my friends!

The videos that always seem to get me are the ones that show people overcoming some type of hardship. I remember one video in particular; it was about a man who had been in an accident that significantly impaired his ability to walk. As the video progressed, you saw him in the hospital, and then you saw him progressing into physical therapy. You saw him constantly lifting weights and being active, even when that meant he was playing basketball while using a wheelchair. Paired with inspirational music that intentionally crescendo throughout the video (gets me every time!), you saw him eventually gain back his ability to walk.

I'll be honest: what gripped me wasn't his transformation, but his focused motivation. After all, even though the video was no more than one or two minutes, his healing process clearly happened over a period of years. There were lots of moments where he was struggling or in pain, but he kept going.

It's hard to keep going when you feel like something crucial in your life is totally absent, isn't it? It's hard to make it through the years of learning how to walk without this thing you thought you'd have by now. And like I've mentioned before, we typically deal with that difficulty by either living in survival mode or becoming overly focused on what we lack, caught in endless conversations about our struggles that quickly descend into a black hole of complaints and negativity. And, with so many words dedicated to talking about our pain, we never seem to have any left to talk about our purpose.

So what is that purpose, you ask? Great question. Alongside "image," Moses uses three other words in Genesis 1:26–28 that would have meant more to Israel than they do to us—*fill, subdue,* and *dominion.* For Israel, this would have connected to the ideas of king and kingdom that were communicated with the word *image.* Specifically, with the instructions given in Genesis 1:28, Israel would have seen that God gave humanity the job of ruling over all of creation on his behalf.

If you were to read the Bible from beginning to end, you would see that it starts in a garden and ends in a city. God designed creation with untapped resources, that we, with our human skill and talent are called to develop. All the innovation that we have seen throughout human history was a part of God's divine plan. He created a world full of potential that you and I are called to mine and cultivate.

But for us to rule over creation on God's behalf means that we have to do it in a way that honors him and points to what we talked about in the last chapter—his character! God loves two things: himself and his creation. So, for us to love God is to love what he loves! We don't just do whatever we want with the responsibilities we have been given; we care for the world with a love that reflects the love we have for God. We also care by reflecting the way God cares for creation. In the same way that he rules, provides, and protects, so should we. This means that this job of ruling over creation really means that we cultivate our little square inch of this world in a way that helps everything and everyone around us thrive. As a gardener tends her flowers to help each one bloom beautifully, so we have been tasked with the responsibility to care about the flourishing of the world.

As you probably already know, our generation is both highly connected and disconnected at the same time. Most of us are accessible twenty-four hours a day because our phones are usually with us at all times. We might not answer our phones at 3:00 a.m., but if we wanted to, we wouldn't have to reach far because many of us sleep with them nearby! With YouTube, Google, Facebook, Instagram, email, and a plethora of apps and other websites, we can talk to anyone anywhere in the world. But even though we have such easy access to one another, there doesn't seem to be any lack of pain or suffering around us.

Sometimes we can think that the "bad" stuff only happens in urban areas, but there is plenty of brokenness in the suburbs and rural areas. Homes with manicured lawns and perfectly organized pantries are full of people who feel broken, lost, and full of despair. They can also be places where addiction runs rampant and family relationships are shattered. The same thing goes for both high-rise apartment buildings and farms in the middle of nowhere. These people are our neighbors, and Genesis 1:26–28 tells us that we should care about what's happening in their lives. But, not only should we care; we are called to do something about it.

Now, you certainly can't bring the good news of the gospel into all of those places of darkness by yourself. But all of us together? We would be unstoppable! Because, . . . when it comes to the proclamation of the gospel, the church is Plan A. There is no Plan B. There is no one else coming to step in for us if we don't do our jobs. But our "cultivation of the earth" work doesn't stop after we evangelize. While the work of salvation is God's alone, he uses us to tell people the truth of the gospel both with our words *and* our lives.

God is redeeming humanity *and* restoring creation. We don't get saved to sit around and wait till we can escape to heaven. Our salvation frees us up to continue the work God designed for us in the garden of Eden. By both preaching the gospel with our words and living out the truth of the gospel in our actions, as image-bearers reflecting the character of God, we get to be a part of this restoration process. Instead of remaining isolated in our own homes or our Christian circles, we venture out into the dark places to bring the light of Christ. Through our spheres of influence and skills and gifting we are able to prioritize the flourishing of others.

This is the purpose Joshua would have been reminded of in his reading of the Book of the Law. This is what would motivate him to face all of what was waiting for him in Canaan. He would fight to overcome obstacle after obstacle because his purpose was greater than his pain. Joshua knew he was part of a bigger story, and it is this purpose that fueled his faithfulness to God.

An Opportunity to Make an Impact

At first glance, the idea of stewarding the world on behalf of God can seem like an overwhelming task. Even more so, it can seem disconnected from our everyday reality. It's one thing for Joshua to have a purpose in God's greater story, but how does that relate to the lives we lead in our day and time?

Every day provides us with a fresh opportunity to remind ourselves that we are part of something bigger. Each day brings with it new possibilities for how we can participate in God's plan of restoration. Our daily tasks go from being merely mundane to divine appointments. Every encounter we have with another image-bearer is an opportunity to help heal their brokenness or create a pathway for them to thrive.

I don't watch a lot of movies, but when I do I tend to watch documentaries. One summer a few years ago I decided to be spontaneous and go see a documentary at one of the artsy theaters in town. On my way into the theater, a woman walked up to me. She quickly began to tell me her story, explaining how she and her family were homeless. Life had dealt them a bad hand, and she just needed some help getting a hotel room for the night so they wouldn't have to sleep on the street. I patiently listened to her story, thinking back to the season of my own life when I was living paycheck to paycheck, struggling to pay my bills.

After she got done sharing, I agreed to help her out. I also used the moment to talk to her about the gospel, making sure she didn't leave without hearing about God. As our conversation came to an end, she offered her gratitude for something I didn't expect. She thanked me for looking her in the eyes while we were talking. For her, my eye contact communicated that I saw her as human, worthy of my attention and compassion. Throughout her experience with homelessness, she was commonly ignored by others. They wouldn't make eye contact or respond to her at all. The denial of this small common courtesy was dehumanizing. So, my efforts to treat her as a fellow image-bearer was extremely meaningful to her and confirmed the truth of the gospel I had shared.

Whether it's our family, coworkers, or the cashier at Target, we all interact with other people on a daily basis. One powerful choice we can make in these interactions is to see the other person as a fellow image-bearer, consider their story, and pray for an opportunity to serve them. By doing this we are immediately reminded that their well-being is our responsibility. Now, this responsibility is not codependency or the enablement of sinful behavior. Rather, it is a desire to help them genuinely thrive in life.

This might come in the form of providing a safe and loving home for a child or free legal aid to a woman caught in the throes of human trafficking. But whatever it may be, it is a task that requires the use of the passions and gifting that God has given to us. A love of home organization is used to help bring calm out of chaos, while a love of medicine is used to help fix physical ailments. Each one of us has a sphere of influence and a specific skill set that God strategically uses to transform the world. But we as individuals aren't responsible for the world; we are just responsible for the pieces that God gives to us. I wonder what yours is.

Sometimes, these pieces will be small, as we face a season of low capacity or difficulty. Yet we can still move toward helping others thrive, whether that be checking in on a neighbor as you go for your daily walk or helping a fellow church member move on a random Saturday afternoon. Other times, these pieces may be big as God calls us together with other believers to accomplish his will on a large scale. Issues like racism, injustice, abortion, and human trafficking might seem overwhelming, but our calling leads us to lean in, not turn away. We educate ourselves, reading books and listening to personal stories. We gather with others, collectively creating strategic plans that will meet the needs of those who are in our care. We live out the truth of the gospel in our kitchens and on the streets of our community, courageously bringing the light of Jesus into dark places.

Prolonged seasons of longing or suffering can crowd our minds and hearts. If we aren't careful, they will consume all of our attention, leaving us no room to envision the new opportunities that each day brings us. We forget the calling on our life, both to image God and care for his world. But, no matter how painful or persistent our longing might be, it is not the entirety of our lives.

Friend, please know that God has so much for you to do. Even when your capacity might seem small, the opportunity to care for the people around you still exists. Many times our pain is the very conduit through which God allows us to make a transformative impact in this world. Our struggles provide us with an invaluable education that allows us to bring hope and healing to another person who is walking through that same situation.

I think of my friend Eillen who serves in a ministry that provides support to women who have lost their children through a miscarriage or still birth. Or my friend Samantha who began a ministry that supports women who are going through seasons of transition, including job loss, homelessness, and divorce. While the ministries they serve in are different, the reason why these two women serve is the same—they've been through it in the past, and they are simply trying to help those who are going through it now. What at one time was a source of longing for them, has been transformed into a source of comfort and love for others.

While it can be painful, our seasons of suffering or longing are not in vain. The possibilities are endless for what God can and will do with them. Our job is to have the willingness to see our seasons with new eyes of hope, realizing that if there is still breath in our bodies, then there is still life for us to live.

Friend, we have some benevolent ruling left to do. We have some cultivation left to dig our hands into. We have some dominion to exercise in this world. What's your square inch? How might you show it what God looks like?

The Practice of Remembrance || Our Divine Identity and Purpose

The spiritual practice of remembering who we are is similar to the practice of remembering God's character and promises—it is hard to remember what we don't know. But it is also hard to think about our calling and impact if we don't give ourselves space with the Holy Spirit to think through these things. So, grab your journal and Bible, and find a quiet space to read through the verses below and answer these few questions with the Lord. Go slow and give time for him to show you the truth about yourself through his Word.

- Genesis 1:27
- 1 Peter 2:9
- Galatians 2:20
- John 15:15–16
- Ephesians 1:7
- Ephesians 2:10

- Philippians 1:6
- Colossians 3:1–4

1. Who do these verses tell you are in Christ? How does that compare with how you currently view yourself?

2. Read John 15:15–16 again. What is the fruit that you believe God has called you to bear? Look up Galatians 5:22–23 to help you with your answer.

3. How might your area of influence (home, work, school, neighborhood) be different if you bore this fruit and helped others to do so?

4. What specific passions, gifts, or skills has God given you, and how might they help you accomplish God's purpose for your life?

As we spend time with God and his Word, he will give us a renewed perspective of who we are in him. But he will also show us how to not only believe this truth, but give us a vision for how we can live it out. This brings us to the next stop on our journey: faith.

Chapter 7

Embrace Faith

Personal affirmations have been helpful for me in my ministry journey. In the words of my mom: "Sometimes you have to encourage yourself!" One affirmation or motto I frequently use is "do it afraid." I don't exactly remember when I came across that phrase. Perhaps I saw it somewhere or maybe I just thought it up on my own. But I do remember the moments when I have said it to myself, like the time I was trying to give myself a pep talk before going to work. I had just started my first ministry job leading the Singles Ministry in my church. It proved to be a role that would help me grow so much, but it also brought out my insecurity and anxiety. With this particular self-pump-up speech, I was sitting in my car about to attend a Bible study led by a group of my volunteers. In my role, I led singles of all different ages, and for some of the folks in this group, I was old enough to be their grand-daughter! Rushing through my mind were thoughts of, "How do I lead someone who has lived so much more life than me?!"

This was my first time meeting them, and to say I was unsure of myself would be an understatement.

During this season, my goal was to learn how to be a good leader. I had responded to God's calling on my life for ministry and was excited about the impact he could make through me. In my mind, the possibilities were endless. But the thing is, no matter how many books you read or courses you take, the only real way to learn how to lead is by doing it. So, as beautiful as my ideas were, the road to accomplish them would be full of obstacles, things that would try to prevent me from moving forward. In order to fulfill the calling on my life, I had to learn how to push past those obstacles and just "do it afraid."

I would go on to build great relationships with those volunteers, but it didn't happen overnight. That Bible study meeting probably ended up being a bit awkward, and some of my fears of being seen as too young for leadership were probably realized. But I kept going back. With each meeting or event, I would tell myself, "Do it afraid." God had so clearly captured my heart with a vision for what was possible, and I knew that the only way to accomplish it would be to keep moving forward. I needed to walk in faith with courage and determination.

Learning from Joshua

Generally, repetition in a passage is a signal that we need to pay attention. Whatever is being said multiple times is really important. In the last few verses of God's message to Joshua,

God repeats the same phrase three times—"be strong and courageous." As he is telling Joshua that his future success is connected to his obedience, God tells him that he will need strength, or more so sheer determination, to accomplish his mission.

Joshua spent his whole life hearing the truth about God and stories of God's continual love and faithfulness for him and Israel. He knew what it was like to live in slavery and he knew what it was like to be free. Joshua had spent forty years in the wilderness helping Moses lead Israel. He had always been able to rely upon Moses, benefiting from his constant leadership and guidance. But things were different now. Moses was gone, and the future of Israel was in the hands of Joshua.

Furthermore, unbeknownst to him, Joshua would spend the next twenty-five years of his life fighting. Like I mentioned in an earlier chapter, Israel would fight against a total of thirty-one kings in their effort to take hold of the land they had been promised. The purpose God had for Joshua would require him to lead his people into battle over and over again. Joshua would have to overcome significant obstacles caused by his own people and by the enemies Israel would fight against.

Some Old Testament scholars believe that at this point in history there are more than two million Israelites waiting to go into the land of Canaan.[1] TWO MILLION! Just pause and think about what it would look like to lead two million people on a journey that includes crossing a major body of water (the Jordan River). My mind is blown thinking about the coordination that type of feat would require.

Following God's commands, Joshua would have to make the necessary tactical decisions to get everyone across the river and give those directions to the twelve tribes of Israel. Under his leadership, TWO MILLION people—men, women, and children—would walk from one side of the river to the other. I get stressed out trying to make sure my emails are worded correctly! I can't imagine the weight Joshua would feel leading all those people through such a major endeavor. It would actually prove to be one in a *long list* of decisions that affected the well-being of Israel. If at any point Joshua failed, people could die. Needless to say, the stakes were high.

His was a future that included an uncharted path to a sure goal. God, in his sovereignty, would ensure that Israel would take over the land they had been promised. But God did not present Joshua with the exact steps of how that would happen. He told him where he was going, how he needed to stay on track, and promised to be with him the whole way. That's it.

So, for Joshua to accomplish his purpose, he would need to step out into the unknown. By faith Joshua needed to use all that God had given him to pursue the future goal God had promised him. But his ability to walk in faith would be supported by two important characteristics: sheer determination and courage.

What Is Faith?

Faith is one of those words Christians use frequently, but when asked to define it we might have difficulty coming up with a succinct statement. When I'm asked to explain the word *faith*, I often use the definition of my former pastor, Dr. Tony Evans. In his words, "Faith is acting like it is so even when it is not so in order that it might be so because God said so."[2] Or as Hebrews 11:1 (NIV) puts it, "Faith is confidence in what we hope for and assurance about what we do not see." More than a feeling, faith is belief that produces action.

More often than not, our belief in Jesus will require us to do something based upon an incomplete set of information. Simply put, God rarely gives us all the details. He will ask us to put aside our need to know or understand everything and just live as if what he said was true. No matter how hard I ask for the details, and I've asked plenty of times, God has routinely made the mission clearer as I've gone along.

I remember moving to Dallas to go to seminary. I tried as hard as I could to get a job before I left Chicago, but was unsuccessful. I earnestly believed that God was leading me to take the step of faith to go to seminary, but I was unsure of how I would survive once I got there. I had a bit of money saved up and a place to sleep. That's it. By conventional wisdom, I shouldn't have stepped foot in Dallas without a job. But I went anyway. And you know what happened? The Lord blessed me with a job that helped pay for my tuition. He ended up blessing me beyond what I could have even imagined was possible. However, the blessing came *after* I took a step of faith, not before. Faith required that I make decisions, trusting in God's leading and in his promises of provision. I didn't know how he was going to work it out, but faith pushed me to live as if he would.

But where does faith come from? you might ask. Is it something we are responsible for experiencing and expressing, or is it something given to us? Like so many other things in Scripture, the answer is not either-or but both-and. On one hand, Scripture tells us that "without faith it is impossible to please him, for whoever would draw near to God must believe that he exists and that he rewards those who seek him" (Heb. 11:6). Therefore, our ability to please God is directly connected to our active belief in him, a belief that is not only in our heads but in our hearts and our feet. We're responsible to express it. On the other hand, though, Ephesians 2:8–9 tells us that by grace we, "have been saved through faith. And this is not your own doing; it is the gift of God, not a result of works, so that no one may boast." So this same faith that we are supposed to embody is also a gift from God. Do you see? There's both a human element and a divine element at play here. Faith is a gift given by God, but expressed by us. Said another way, God gives us the thing that pleases him—he gives us the muscle of faith, if you will. But we are called to exercise that gift in everyday moments.

This is such good news! Sometimes it can be hard to walk in faith, trusting God with our feet. In these moments it is a comfort to know that God gifts us with the faith we need. In fact, he was invested in giving us faith before we even knew we needed it. By the power of the Holy Spirit, God gives us the ability to believe in him, and it is this same ability by which we are able to live out the very truth we believe. By faith we came to Christ at the moment of our conversion—a gift given to us by God!—and by faith we walk with him every step of the journey after that moment.

What Is Determination?

In the original language, the phrase "be strong" denotes the ability to accomplish the intended mission. So when God tells Joshua to "be strong," he is telling him he needs a firm determination to reach the goal no matter what gets in his way. With millions of people under his care, I'm more than sure Joshua had plenty of things, and people, trying to block him from accomplishing his goal.

Whether it is your kids, your small group, or yourself, leading people is hard. Outside of decision-making, loneliness, conflict, and the joy of being misunderstood usually accompany any leadership position. Along with these external struggles comes the struggles of our own heart and mind—depression, anxiety, and doubt. The joys of leadership are many, but the sorrows are many as well. Joshua would lead Israel to accomplish glorious things, but these accomplishments would not be without hardship and pain.

Determination is a single-minded focus that is fueled by our faith in God. It is the internal push that helps us continue walking in faith when things get hard. When I think of determination, I always think of one of those inflatable punching bags. No matter how hard you hit it, the bag always pops back up.

While a life that revolves around longing is weighty and frustrating, it is familiar. We've learned how to manage the pain, whether we choose to avoid it or numb it. But for some of us, moving past our pain is new, undiscovered territory. We don't know what will happen if we choose to change our mindset and show up differently. To make things harder, change rarely happens immediately; it usually takes time. This means that in our attempts to live based upon the truth we believe about God and ourselves, we will inevitably get knocked down.

Most of the time the culprits for these attacks are discouragement and despair. We are all familiar with their M.O.—softly whispering lies in our ears until we crumble under the weight of their deception. But, like a boxing coach in the ring, determination jumps in, pulls us up off the ground, and tells us to get back in the game. It reminds us that no matter what, the way forward is better.

If the apostle Paul had a middle name, I think it would be Determination. He experiences an inordinate amount of obstacles during his missionary journeys. More than once he is attacked by a mob and experiences physical violence in response to his evangelistic efforts. But as we read about it in the book of Acts, it seems as if every time he gets beat up, he just gets back up and goes to the next town. In 2 Corinthians 11:24–27 he even details for us all the hardship he experienced. He writes,

> Five times I received at the hands of the Jews
> the forty lashes less one. Three times I was
> beaten with rods. Once I was stoned. Three
> times I was shipwrecked; a night and a day I

was adrift at sea; on frequent journeys, in danger from rivers, danger from robbers, danger from my own people, danger from Gentiles, danger in the city, danger in the wilderness, danger at sea, danger from false brothers; in toil and hardship, through many a sleepless night, in hunger and thirst, often without food in cold and exposure.

Yet, when he talks about how he views his hardships in 2 Corinthians 4:7–18, Paul writes this:

But we have this treasure in jars of clay, to show that the surpassing power belongs to God and not to us. We are afflicted in every way, but not crushed; perplexed, but not driven to despair; persecuted, but not forsaken; struck down, but not destroyed; always carrying in the body the death of Jesus, so that the life of Jesus may also be manifested in our bodies. For we who live are always being given over to death for Jesus' sake, so that the life of Jesus also may be manifested in our mortal flesh. So death is at work in us, but life in you. Since we have the same spirit of faith according to what has been written, "I believed, and so I spoke," we also believe, and so we also speak, knowing that he who raised the Lord Jesus will raise us also with Jesus and bring us with you into his presence. For it is all for your sake, so that as grace extends to more and more people it may increase thanksgiving, to the glory of God. So we do not lose heart. Though our outer self is wasting away, our inner self is being renewed day by day. For this light momentary affliction is preparing for us an eternal weight of glory beyond all comparison, as we look not to the things that are seen but to the things that are unseen. For the things that are seen are transient, but the things that are unseen are eternal.

No matter what happened to Paul, he had a determination that was greater than his pain. He was motivated by the potential of what God could do through him, rather than by what he might suffer doing the work of the Lord.

If this was not enough, Paul also writes about his suffering with a "thorn in his side." No one knows what this thorn is; some say a medical condition, others say a relational one. Regardless of the specifics, Paul prayed earnestly for the Lord to take it away. The Lord didn't. Yet, even this did not discourage Paul; he saw this as another opportunity to bring glory to God. Even when faced with death (2 Cor. 1:8–9), Paul was unbothered, seeing it as an opportunity to experience the resurrecting power of God. Every time Paul got knocked down, he seemed to pop right back up.

If we were to look at Paul's story in its entirety, I think we would see two key motivations that are behind his determination. First, Paul knew what was at stake. After encountering

Jesus, he had come to a clear understanding of God and the mission he had to accomplish. Paul knew that his mission had an eternal impact, for him the cost of people not hearing the gospel was greater than the pain he experienced while sharing it.

Second, Paul had a vision for what could be if he accomplished the mission God had given him, and it wasn't just a vision of his thorn going away or life feeling warm and comfortable. He had a heart that was captured by the reality of lives being transformed by the gospel. What does this mean? It means that the mission of God captured his imagination even more than the fulfilment of his personal longings. It's not that his thorn didn't matter. Surely it did, or the Bible wouldn't record him bringing it before the Lord for relief. It's that he was captivated by something greater. He had seen miracles, healings, people turning away from cult worship and old patterns of Judaism. Paul knew what it was like to raise someone from the dead! Paul knew the power of a transformed life and the greater impact his efforts could have on the evangelization of the world. Part of the reason you and I had the privilege of hearing the gospel is because of the faithfulness of Paul. His determination helped prepare the way for *our* spiritual transformation.

Our ability to make real the possibilities that hope stirs within us requires determination. Fueled by our trust in God, we are also motivated by a vision for the potential impact of our actions. Even if the life transformed is only our own, this benefit far outweighs any cost we might endure achieving it.

What Is Courage?

Whenever someone talks about Black History or the Civil Rights Movement, there is a predictable list of people they might mention. Names like Martin Luther King Jr., Harriet Tubman, or Frederick Douglass are commonplace in these conversations. With a list that is usually short, there are many important people who get overlooked. One of these people is Fannie Lou Hamer.

Born in 1917, Hamer and her family grew up in Mississippi picking cotton. Like many Black people during that time period, Hamer grew up poor under the weight of a segregated society steeped in racism. Eventually her experience in the South would lead her to become an advocate for human rights, specifically fighting for Black people to have the right to vote. However, her efforts were often met with opposition and violence.

In her famous speech at the 1964 Democratic National Convention, Fannie Lou Hamer recounted an experience she had after attending a voter registration workshop in South Carolina. She and her friends had stopped at a bus depot and decided to sit in the "white only" area. The police chief responded by ordering them to the "colored" area, but they refused since segregation had just been deemed illegal. Hamer and her friends ended up being arrested and taken to the county jail. During their time in custody, they were brutally beaten. So much so, that Hamer lost vision in one of her eyes and suffered permanent kidney damage. Needless to say, the merciless beating was meant to evoke fear, dissuading Hamer and her friends from pursuing their fight for integration and the right to vote.

The thing is, the beating ended up having the opposite effect. Instead of crumbling under the weight of fear, Hamer and her friends chose to fight harder on behalf of other humans made in the image of God. After this event, Fannie Lou Hamer would go on to be a major figure in American history, as she continued organizing voter registration events and remained active in civil rights causes until her death.[3]

What always inspires me about Hamer's story is her courage. Knowing that her actions might lead to additional violence or her death, Hamer kept going. If you read about her, you will hear her unwavering hope for a better life—both for herself and other Black people. Even when faced with death, for her, the cost of retreating far outweighed the benefit.

Courage pushes past fear. It is a strength that gives us the ability to withstand danger or difficulty. While the opposition we face might not be as severe as what Fannie Lou Hamer experienced, walking in faith will present us plenty of hurdles to overcome.

For instance, the one thing most of us fear is the prospect of our situation never changing. It's the fear that we will never get married or the healing we desire never showing up. But what is usually attached to this fear is a clouded imagination. We have a difficult time imagining a life that is both joyful and devoid of the things we desperately desire. Even if we manage to see the open doors around us, we can be held back by the belief that our life won't be any better if we choose to walk through them.

In addition to fear of unmet expectations, we can be fearful of the obstacles that stand between us and our first step of faith. Many times, the biggest hurdles to our personal transformation are the people around us. While well-meaning, a parent, friend, or spouse can lack the faith we are trying to live by. As we are growing in our ability to trust God, they remain skeptical. Whatever dreams we have for newness they can crush with their pessimism. Or for others, our choice to embrace our longing can look to them like a lack of faith. In their mind, we should just try harder, not accepting anything less than exactly what we have prayed for.

Left to its own devices, fear can be a powerful motivator. We don't want to experience the consequences that fear is telling us will happen when we choose to move forward. The reality of experiencing what we fear can be overwhelming for us. But over the years I have found that the best way to deal with fear is not to run from it, but walk right through it. We have to face it head-on and line up our fears next to what is always greater—the character of God.

Fear tends to leave out some details when it tries to "caution" us from walking in faith. It won't remind you of God's presence. It won't remind you of his sovereign power, his ability to work things out on your behalf and to fight your battles for you. It won't remind you of his promised provision, his ability to give you exactly what you need at the very moment you need it. Fear will have you thinking you are walking alone, with no power and no resources. The goal of fear is for you to forget God, thinking that your ability to walk in faith depends on you alone.

But the Bible gives us a different approach. There are two different kinds of fear the Bible mentions. The first type of fear is a reverence for God. While important, that's not the kind of fear I'm talking about. I'm referencing the second kind—a fear of danger that prevents us from living out the calling that God has placed on our lives. Below are a few verses that speak to how we ought to deal with this second kind of fear:

- "Even though I walk through the valley of the shadow of death, I will fear no evil, for you are with me; your rod and your staff, they comfort me" (Ps. 23:4).

- "The LORD is my light and my salvation; whom shall I fear? The Lord is the stronghold of my life; of whom shall I be afraid?" (Ps. 27:1).

- "Fear not, for I am with you; be not dismayed, for I am your God; I will strengthen you, I will help you, I will uphold you with my righteous right hand" (Isa. 41:10).

- "But seek first the kingdom of God and his righteousness, and all these things will be added to you. Therefore do not be anxious about tomorrow, for tomorrow will be anxious for itself. Sufficient for the day is its own trouble" (Matt. 6:33–34).

- "Peace I leave with you; my peace I give to you. Not as the world gives do I give to you.

Let not your hearts be troubled, neither let them be afraid" (John 14:27).

- "For God gave us a spirit not of fear but of power and love and self-control" (2 Tim. 1:7).

What is interesting is that each of these verses uses the same method to talk about fear. They all point the reader back to the character of God. Fear is a real emotion that we will feel while trying to walk in faith. There are a lot of uncertainties when we decide to make a change in our lives based on the prompting of the Lord. As people who have lived with longing for an extended season, we are also used to being disappointed. We fear trying something new only to be left off worse than we started. But when what we are moving forward in is the call of God on our lives, we must remember that to move forward is simply to live in light of the story of redemption that is already in motion.

Now, notice my choice of words. I didn't say "when we are moving forward in our own plans and preferences." I said, "when we are moving forward *in the call of God.*" There are plenty of ways we can "move forward" in ways that aren't actually forward at all, and determination in those paths will only bring us harm. For example, to escape our pain, we can run to a terrible relationship that we know is not honoring to the Lord, nor in line with the ways he tells us to approach romantic relationships, and we'll inevitably get burned. Or we can start spending crazy amounts of money in ways that are not wise, which can end up ruining our ability to let that money flow to others in their times of need. When I speak of moving forward, I'm talking about answering the call to better reflect God in the world, to care for those around you in his name, to bring the gospel to your corner of the world, to take a risk on something his Word clearly values and asks you to live out.

Where fear would tell us that we are taking too big of a risk, the Bible tells us something different. It shows us that the biggest risk has already been taken by God himself through the person and work of Jesus Christ. The only reason we can walk forward in courage is ultimately because of what God has already done for us. The way forward is not a "get rich quick scheme"; it is an opportunity for us to live in the abundant life that Jesus makes available to us. It is a life that is lived based upon the truth of God's character and our identity in him. It is a life that does not minimize our pain, but brings it before him in a posture of lament. It is a life that reminds us that as long as we are connected to him, there is always hope! Courage helps us push past the fear. Even when we feel scared, courage enables us to "do it afraid" because we realize we aren't alone. God goes with us every time. He's there to hear our cries. He's there to give us faith. He's there to push us forward. If these things are true, and they are, there's no road scary enough to hold us back!

How They All Work Together

If you have read through the story of Moses, you probably noticed that he went through several unusual experiences with Israel. As I'm reading through them, I am usually saying to myself, "Yo, this really happened!!" My favorite one of these stories happens in Exodus 17:8–13. Israel was fighting a nation called Amalek. Moses, Aaron, and Hur goes up on top of a hill to watch the battle play out. As long as Moses's hands stayed up, Israel would be winning. But anytime his hands came down, Amalek would begin to overtake Israel. Moses tried his hardest to keep his hands up, but eventually he got tired. When this happened, Aaron and Hur jumped in and began holding up his hands. Even though Moses had become weary, Aaron and Hur were not. With their assistance, Moses was able to accomplish his goal, which enabled Israel to accomplish theirs—winning the battle against Amalek.

Walking in faith is beautiful and hard. Living based upon the truth of God's character and our identity can be exhilarating because we are part of a larger story. We have to learn how to tell the time in light of where Scripture says we exist in the bigger story of God's work in the world. For instance, it's not just Thursday; it's Thursday in redemptive history, in a story where Jesus came but has not yet returned.[4]

As we wait on his return we embrace the life we have been given. We walk forward in faith knowing that when we get weary, determination and courage will be there to hold our arms up. Fueled by God himself, this powerful duo helps us to push past any obstacles we might encounter as we fight to achieve the goal that God has set before us. Because ultimately, like Joshua, we can only "be strong and courageous" because the Lord our God is with us wherever we go.

The Practice of Faith

Now, you may be saying, "This is all great, Elizabeth, but how do I actually take the first step?"

I'm glad you asked!

First, any conversation about change for people who are navigating extended seasons of longing or suffering needs to be done with a great deal of sensitivity. Different life seasons or circumstances provide different opportunities to each of us. We each have a different set of life variables, including independence, health, finances, and geographic limitations. Yet, within this I believe we can all do something, even if it is a mindset shift (which is neither simple nor small).

For all of us, there is a step of faith we can take to move closer to the joy that is available to all of us through our life with Christ. So, in light of this, taking a step of faith includes four things: *imagining the possibilities, making a plan, confirming the plan in prayer, and inviting the voices of godly counsel.*

I. Imagining the Possibilities

Like I've said before, longing clouds our imagination. We have a hard time seeing what's possible because we are so focused on what isn't possible. As you begin to remind yourself of the bigger story you are a part of, take some time to imagine (with God) what he might have for you to do in this season of life. We all have a set of passions and gifting. Those have not been given to you randomly. God's specific purpose for our lives is usually connected to those two things.

I think of my friend Renee. She grew up in a home where her mom would regularly take in foster children. Growing up, Renee was always in an environment that was focused on investing in the lives of children. Fast-forward to today, and Renee is a foster parent. Even though she is single, she has a passion for helping children in need. In order to become a foster parent, she had to go through several classes, certifications, and interviews. Then, when she was connected with a child, their relationship was rocky at first. But Renee pressed through all of it because her focus was on the greater good of helping children in need.

Take the time to consider how God has wired you, gifted you, and what story he has given you. All of those things matter. Then, in prayer, imagine how you might live out your calling of reflecting God's character and helping other image-bearers flourish. What are your gifts? Your strengths? Your passions? Parts of your story that stand out? Opportunities you've been given? Spheres of influence? Record these, and then think of what sorts of good work could intersect these things. Come up with a list! You aren't committing to any of them, you're just dreaming at this stage.

2. Making a Plan

Ideas are great, but they usually stay ideas unless we are intentional about creating a plan. Again, what I'm suggesting is not a 100-step business plan for how you are going to take over the world! Sometimes we can be overwhelmed by what change requires. But I've learned that we can usually find one thing to move us one step closer to our goal. So narrow down your imagination list to two ideas. Then decide on one thing you can do to start working on one of them. Maybe your idea is to be more grateful, so you decide to create a gratitude jar. Or, for those who are more ambitious, you decide to pursue the degree you have been putting off for a long time. So, step number one is figuring out how to apply! Change happens one step at a time, so whether the step is big or small, it is moving you closer to your goal.

3. Confirming the Plan in Prayer

While we have great ideas, sometimes the Lord will point us in a different direction or make our good ideas even better. God should be a part of your entire process, but praying before we take action reminds us of whose story we are living in, and lining up our plans with Scripture allows us to ensure we are walking according to his ways and not our own. Our faith is not in ourselves, our ingenuity, or personal strength. The faith we walk by is rooted in God!

4. Inviting the Voices of Godly Counsel

If you're having trouble coming up with any of this, invite some seasoned and godly voices to help you along. Sometimes we need others to help us remember our strengths or point out opportunities for service that we've potentially missed. Other times, the problem is not that we don't know what to do; it's that we *do* know what to do, but need some godly folks around us to hold us accountable to our one small step! Inviting in the wisdom of others helps us not to go at things alone. Consider who in your life might be a good, godly source of wisdom and help as you embrace faith for the next step in your journey.

As we lament our longing and allow God to stir our hearts with hope, our faith is revitalized. We come to realize that the story we are a part of is bigger than our pain, and within it is a purpose for us that is sure. So, we jump in with courage and determination by our side, remembering that no matter what happens, the way forward is better.

Chapter 8

Embrace Joy

nyone who knows me knows I love home decor and can regularly be found in the home section of Target or at a Home Goods store! Over the years I have curated a collection of art, music, and general decor pieces that tell the story of my travels and adventures. Each piece serves as a memory of an event or season of life. But some of my decor pieces serve as a memory of specific people. One of those pieces is a set of small stuffed elephants. My old roommate Diane loved elephants, and I got them to remind me of her.

Over a decade ago, Diane and I shared an apartment a few blocks away from the place we both worked. She was a friend who was also a mentor. Diane taught me so much about what it meant to lead and love people well. Since I was a new manager, she helped me navigate difficult staff issues as well as learn to advocate for my own professional development. If I wasn't at my desk, I could usually be found in her office laughing, talking, and gleaning from the overflow of her wisdom.

Our roommate arrangement only lasted a few months, and not too long after I moved out, Diane fell on hard times. The emotional weight of bad romantic relationships, significant job changes, and the general struggles of life took their toll on her.

I'll never forget when I heard the news about her passing. I was devastated. Life had become too much for my friend Diane, and she chose to respond by taking her own life. For a long time, I mourned Diane's death. I spent hours thinking deeply about her life and the choices she had made. I grieved all that would not be and the moments in my life she would not be a part of.

Honestly, my friend gave up on life. Overwhelmed by despair, joy for her was nowhere to be found. Perhaps her decisions felt irreversible to her, or maybe the opinions of others who watched her make those decisions became too much for her to bear. All I know is that my mentor decided that ending her life would be easier than fighting to find a reason for living. She chose to give up rather than fight for joy.

I got those elephants to remind me of Diane, both the life she lived and her choice to commit suicide. I did it not only to remember her, but also to remember to never give up. No matter how elusive it might feel or far away it might seem, I wanted to be a person who fought to find and hold onto joy, even in the midst of sorrow.

Where Do We Find Joy?

Joy is the one thing we want in a season of longing. But many of us consider it unattainable, close enough to see it but far away enough to be just out of reach. After a season of suffering, we can start to see joy as the privilege of the naive. It is evidence of a life that has been unscathed by the sharp edges of the world. Once our eyes are opened to what life is really like, joy becomes like an absentee father. It shows up every so often, but doesn't stay for long.

In our minds, our heart has a one-room occupancy. So if we are experiencing sorrow, we think there is no room for joy. If anything, joy becomes the mask we wear to cover up the sadness and pain we feel on the inside.

If that wasn't enough, our joy problems can be further exacerbated by the shallow answers we hear from well-meaning people. Far too often we are given easy answers for complex problems, told that *"it will all work out," "God will never give you more than you can handle,"* or *"maybe God is trying to get your attention."* The truth is, sometimes it doesn't work out, the weight of our longing feels like God has given us *way* more than we can handle, and the pain still flows long after he's gotten our attention. When the joy that is delivered to us on the back of easy answers fails, it can be hard to know where to find it.

Learning from Israel (and Russell)

While seemingly elusive, joy for the Christian is not as inaccessible as we might believe. In fact, the joy we see discussed in Scripture comes from the mouths of those who knew deep sorrow and suffering. With Joshua as our guide, much of this book has been dedicated to talking about the life of Israel. Even though Joshua was responsible for leading them into the land of Canaan, his formative struggles would also be formative struggles for Israel. The entire nation had been enslaved in Egypt. They had all cried out to God for deliverance and seen the deliverance come. But long after Joshua had gone to be with the Lord, we will see Israel continue to struggle. They would experience seasons of great prosperity and they would also experience seasons of great tragedy. Yet through it all, Israel would be a people who chose joy.

Much of the Old Testament tells the history of Israel. Even the book of Joshua recounts historical events that connect the dots between Genesis 1 and Jesus. But there are a few books that create a bit of an interlude. They aren't telling a story per se, but sharing about what Israel experienced as their story unfolded. Specifically, in the book of Psalms we read about Israel's experience of living life with God. Some of these psalms were written by Moses, during the time of Joshua. But most of them were written long after Joshua had died. Yet, the leadership of Joshua would have been a significant root in the tree of Israel's joy, because for them, joy was a present state of being that was grounded in their past experiences.

Psalm 126 is one of the Psalms of Ascent, written after Israel was released from exile. Hundreds and hundreds of years after Joshua brought Israel into the land, they would be kicked out by God. After being persistent in their disobedience, God would use foreign nations to chastise them. He would allow the Babylonians to attack Israel, destroy their beloved Jerusalem, and take them back to Babylon as prisoners of war. For seventy years, Israel would live in exile under Babylon's rule. Eventually, God would show them grace and allow them to go home. Those folks were the ones who wrote Psalm 126 as a song of ascent—one of many in a group of songs (Pss. 120–134) sung by the people of God as they made their pilgrimage to Jerusalem each year for three annual festivals (Passover, Pentecost, and the Day of Atonement).

> When the LORD restored the fortunes of
> Zion,
> we were like those who dream.
> Then our mouth was filled with laughter,
> and our tongue with shouts of joy;
> then they said among the nations,
> "The LORD has done great things for them."
> The LORD has done great things for us;
> we are glad.
>
> Restore our fortunes, O LORD,
> like streams in the Negeb!
> Those who sow in tears
> shall reap with shouts of joy!
> He who goes out weeping,

bearing the seed for sowing,
shall come home with shouts of joy,
bringing his sheaves with him.
(Ps. 126)

Containing only a few verses, this psalm can be split into two basic parts. In verses 1–3, Israel expresses joy because of their deliverance from exile. In verse 4–6, Israel offers a prayer to God asking for a future restoration of everyone who had been taken into captivity. The interesting thing is that in both sections, joy is intermixed with a recognition of the hard things they had, and still were, experiencing. When Israel came home, they came back to a demolished city and desolate farmland. Starting over for them would be no easy feat. But in the midst of all of this they could still rejoice. While they were trying to put the pieces of their life back together, they praised the God who made their season of transition possible.

Israel's joy was not shallow and did not ignore their current realities. On the contrary, it transcended above them. Their joy found its strength in the past, not the present. Israel's words of delight reflected a celebration of past deliverance coupled with a future hope for an experience of the same.

I have been to quite a few types of churches over the years. Some have been predominantly white; others have been predominantly black. I have been to the church that met for three hours on Sunday, took a break to eat dinner, and then came back for a two-hour Sunday night service. I have also been to the church that managed to pack announcements, worship, a sermon, and communion into a 55-minute service.

I've been to churches that had a full band, choir, and several skilled tambourine players in the audience. I've also been to the church where praise and worship was led by one guy on a guitar singing acoustic worship songs. When it comes to church in America, I haven't seen it all, but I have seen a lot!

Yet, even in my diverse experience, I never met anyone as expressive during worship as Russell. When it was time for praise and worship, Russell would find his spot up front and dance as if no one was looking. There was a freedom you felt radiate from him. You knew he didn't care what anyone was thinking. He was unbothered by the judgmental opinions of the church folks who were watching him!

One Sunday I found myself in a conversation with Russell. I don't know how we got to chatting, but quickly into our conversation he began telling me his story. Growing up without a father, he had made some bad choices as a teenager that eventually led him to several years of homelessness, drug use, and incarceration. Thankfully, the church didn't reject him but pursued him. Their love for him eventually led him to get sober. Russell told me that he was now trying to get back on his feet, looking for a job and a permanent place to stay. He then proceeded to tell me about his "dancing." Maybe he knew I wondered why he was so expressive during worship or maybe he just wanted to talk about it. Either way, he began answering all the questions I had in my mind but had never asked.

Russell knew what it was like to hit rock bottom. He knew what it was like to feel hopeless, not knowing how his situation was going to change. He knew what it was like to try to get sober only to relapse and fall back into his patterns of drug addiction. Russell was familiar with experiencing prolonged seasons of longing. His was a desire for sobriety and stability that eluded him for a long time. But one day, someone told Russell about Jesus. He heard the truth about a God who loved him, died to save him, and offered him new life. That day proved to be the first day of a new life for him. After getting saved, Russell eventually got sober and found his way back to church.

This is why Russell worshiped God through dance. Every chance he got, he rejoiced in what God had done for him. Even though life carried more than a little difficulty for him, his joy remained steady because his joy was in the past faithfulness of the Lord.

When we feel that joy is elusive, it's usually because we have a hard time finding joy in our current circumstances. Frankly, we might feel that with our current situation there is nothing to be happy about. But the problem isn't that joy is hard to find; it's that we are looking for it in the wrong place. Like Israel and my friend Russell, the roots of our joy aren't in the present but in the past.

Joy as a Counterweight

Dr. Scott Swain, a seminary president and professor of systematic theology, uses two metaphors to talk about the heart. He talks about the heart as a cup and the heart as a scale. He writes, "It seems that folks sometimes offer biblical encouragements—platitudes like 'fear not,' 'do not be

anxious,' and so on—as if the heart were a cup full of fear or
anxiety that needs to be emptied of those emotions so it can
be filled with alternative emotions. But this is wrongheaded."[1]
Swain goes on to explain how this invalidates the appropriateness of certain emotions, such as sorrow or anxiety. Even
though they might be deemed as negative, these emotions are
necessary as they help us express the reality of our pain and
loss. For him, seeing the heart as needing to be emptied of
these emotions is the wrong perspective.

Rather than a cup, Swain suggests we should see the heart
as a balance scale. In this metaphor, the pain we feel rests as a
weight on one side of the scale. Biblical encouragement then
serves as a counterweight, "providing consolations that enable
our hearts to bear the weights of sorrow, anxiety, and fear in
this vale of tears (Ps. 84:6)—until we arrive at our destination
of unmixed, unshakable beatitude in the presence of the triune
God (Ps. 84:4)."[2] For him, the goal is not to remove the hard
emotions but to place them in relation to a larger story: the
reality of God's sovereignty, presence, and work of redemption
in our life.

Swain's insight helps us understand why joy can seem hard
to find—it's because we believe our heart is a cup that can only
be filled with one emotion at a time, a reservoir where joy can't
exist alongside longing. And so in order to truly experience
joy, we think we have to get rid of our longing. Seeing it as
blocking the way to joy, we spin our wheels trying to change
our situation. While some of our efforts produce results, many
times we end up more frustrated because of the lack of fruit
our actions have borne. Because one of the distinguishing

characteristics of longing is that it tends to be something that we can't control.

Rather than seeing longing as blocking our joy, we should see joy as the counterweight to our longing. It points us to truth that helps us bear the weight of our sorrow, allowing our perspective of our longing to be seen through the lens of our joy. Because when joy and sorrow rest on the scale of our heart together and each side is weighed, the biblical promise we can take to the bank is that true joy weighs more, lifting the weight of the sorrow and helping us bear it.

Our Joy Is in Jesus

As we have seen through the life of Israel, and my friend Russell, our joy does not come from our current circumstances. It finds its roots in God, specifically in his past work of faithfulness. It rests in a truth that remains steady even when our current life does not. For us as believers on the other side of the cross, this truth is the truth about salvation in Jesus.

The story of the Bible tells us that we were created to live in community with God. When our eternal community with him was at stake because of sin, he stepped in to restore it. Like Israel, you and I have been delivered too. Except that we were not slaves in Egypt but slaves to sin. The apostle Paul tells us that "he has delivered us from the domain of darkness and transferred us to the kingdom of his beloved Son, in whom we have redemption, the forgiveness of sins" (Col. 1:13–14). We were once enemies of God, powerless to restore the broken community we had with him. But God, being rich in mercy, because of the great love with which he loved us, even when we were dead in our trespasses, made us alive together with Christ—by grace [we] have been saved (Eph. 2:4–5)!

Friend, this is where your joy is found! Over two thousand years ago, Jesus stepped in to save us from the worst kind of longing we could ever experience—a life separate from God. Our joy is fixed in the past reality of his redemption, but it is also fixed in a future reality of this redemption's consummation. We as Christians believe that one day Jesus is returning, to fix all that is broken about this world. He will wipe every tear from our eyes once and for all (Rev. 21:4). Our joy rests in the truth of our unhindered communion with God and in the unwavering truth that one day we will spend eternity with him in a world without sin and longing.

Joy is an emotional state of being that is both a gift from God and a mindset we choose to embody. Like the other biblical tensions we discussed, God is involved in our ability to walk in joy but asks that we be involved too. Here is what the New Testament tells us about joy:

- "These things I have spoken to you, that my joy may be in you, and that your joy may be full" (John 15:11).
- "May the God of hope fill you with all joy and peace in believing, so that by the power of the Holy Spirit you may abound in hope" (Rom. 15:13).
- "Count it all joy, my brothers, when you meet trials of various kinds, for you know

that the testing of your faith produces stead-
fastness" (James 1:2–3).

- "But the fruit of the Spirit is love, joy, peace,
  patience, kindness, goodness, faithfulness,
  gentleness, self-control; against such things
  there is no law" (Gal. 5:22–23).

So, while it can seem hard to find joy, the truth is that it is readily available for all believers. But we don't find it by looking at our present circumstances, we find it by looking at the past work of Jesus and the future hope we have in him!

Friend, please don't miss this! Our ability to experience joy is not blocked by the present pain of our longing. Unlike happiness, joy is not dependent on our circumstances, but transcends above them. It is rooted in our deep understanding of what it means for us to be children of God. Salvation through Jesus Christ changes our present reality and our eternal future. Through Jesus we get access to God and all that he has for us. We get the help of the Holy Spirit, a listening ear for our lament, a hope for future transformation, and a divine identity and purpose through which God will change us and help change the world. Oftentimes, we can be guilty of treating joy as if it has wandered off to some distant place. But the truth is, our *Joy* has always been with us. We just need the eyes to see it.

The Practice of Joy

For one leading expert (Brené Brown) who conducted a study on joy, the relationship between gratitude and joy is undeniable. After gathering 11,000 points of data over the span of twelve years, guess what the result of the study was? There was not *one* person who described themselves as joyful who did not practice gratitude.[3] Said another way, every single person in the study who described themselves as joyful practiced gratitude. While discussing her findings, Brown shares about how she was "startled by the fact that research participants consistently described both joyfulness and gratitude as spiritual practices that were bound to a belief in human connectedness and a power greater than us."[4] Even though all of her research participants would not claim to be Christians, they recognize a truth that is deeply biblical—joy is cultivated through celebratory remembrance.

While we can find pleasure and delight in everyday things, joy is an emotional state of being that transcends above all of our circumstances. It is a posture or way of life that remains steady because it is rooted in something that never moves. Now, even though I believe that joy is a gift from God, I don't think we are precluded from cultivating the gift. Our experience of joy is connected to our habits of spiritual formation.

But discipleship isn't neutral; you won't accidentally grow to reflect the character of God. Even though God is present in the process, our spiritual formation requires intentionality (Phil. 2:12–13). And, we know what it is like to be intentional because we make intentional choices every day. Each morning we wake up, grab coffee, get ready for the day, and probably make some time to scroll through social media. Some of us are in the habit of working out, and some of us, like me, are not. But, whether we realize it or not, we are the sum of our habits. Every day we are being formed into a particular kind of person. Either we are being formed to reflect our culture or we are being formed to reflect Christ.

So, similar to the practice of lament, hope, and remembrance, the practice of joy is an intentional way to celebrate the blessings of God. It helps us remember God as the source of our joy and consistently remember the ways in which he is blessing us. It pushes back against the current of skepticism and disillusionment, bringing our eyes and hearts back to truth that can be easy to forget.

Two ways I believe we can cultivate joy is by regularly practicing gratitude and celebration:

I. Gratitude

Adele Calhoun defines *gratitude* as "a loving and thankful response toward God for his presence with us and within this world. Though 'blessings' can move us into gratitude, it is not at the root of a thankful heart. Delight in God and his good will is the heartbeat of thankfulness."[5] The only steady and unchanging thing in this world is God. So, our joy is ultimately fixed in him. Gratitude gives us a daily opportunity to remind ourselves of the ways that we have experienced God and his blessings. It makes us pause and consider the multitude of ways in which God cares for us through his tangible demonstrations of love.

Whether it's with a gratitude jar, journaling, or through prayer, the habit of seeing the presence of God at work in our lives, and the world, is transformative. We grow to become aware of the abundance of gifts, benefits, mercies, and graces that have been poured into our life. We begin to see what we have more quickly than what we don't have. Our value of the people around us increases as we regularly express how much we appreciate who they are to us or someone else. But most of all, we will grow to know and deeply appreciate the never-ending presence of God in our lives.[6] I wonder, what might practicing gratitude on a regular basis look like for you?

2. Celebration

While similar to gratitude, celebration is a way of engaging in actions that set our hearts toward a posture of worship, praise, and thanksgiving. Celebration helps us create special moments to glorify God for his presence in our lives and work in the world. These celebrations can be big or small, formal or informal. The significance is not necessarily in the amount of detailed planning we do, but in the time we set aside to remember the goodness of God in a special way.

Our celebrations might take the form of a BBQ in our backyard or a picnic in the park. We might turn on some praise music and, like my friend Russell, dance as if no one is watching. Whatever we choose to do, it should be full of praise and worship to God! If for nothing else, we should regularly find time to glorify the Lord, because he is good, his steadfast love endures forever, and his faithfulness to all generations (Ps. 100:5).

Ultimately, both gratitude and celebration cultivate within our hearts the joy we've been given by God. Calhoun captures the heart of this connection when she says,

> To set our hearts on this joy reminds us that we choose how we respond in any particular moment. We can search for God in all circumstances, or not. We can seek the pulse of hope and celebration because it's God's reality. Heaven is celebrating. Right now the cherubim, seraphim, angels, archangels, prophets, apostles, martyrs, and all the company

of saints overflow with joy in the presence of their Creator. Every small experience of Jesus with us is a taste of the joy that is to come. We are not alone—and that in itself is a reason to celebrate.[7]

Friend, as you wrestle with the hardships of this life, remember that joy serves as a counterweight on the scale of your heart. It reminds you that your sorrows are real, but they are also temporary. Joy gives you the perspective and the strength to weather the storms of life. And it also protects you from the pull of habits that seek to block you from seeing the good you truly do have. Rooted in the past and looking toward the future, joy is available to all believers, because we celebrate the glory of God both now and for eternity.

Embrace Your Life

I am the youngest of two children. Growing up, my family moved around a lot, so over the years my sister and I became pretty close. We have a lot of shared experiences, having gone to the same college and both working in the field of education. But another one of our shared experiences is singleness. (Well, my sister is currently married, but she got married in her late twenties.) Growing up in the church like I did, my sister experienced all the bad messaging and unfair pressures that women experience. She knew what it was like to be valued for a role, rather than for who you were as an image-bearer. So during her relationship with her now-husband, my sister would share valuable insight with me. But what she shared wasn't all the gossipy details of her relationship, but a perspective that would shape how I view singleness and marriage. I'll never forget when my sister told me, "Elizabeth, marriage isn't better; it's just different."

To some, these words might seem to be stating an obvious fact. But to me they were profound. The difference my sister was referring to was the costs and the benefits related to single-ness and marriage. She would expound upon this idea years later by using a deck of playing cards to illustrate the dynam-ics of our lives. Now, I love a good illustration. So when she started explaining her playing cards metaphor, I was all ears!

What my sister told me was that life is like a game that uses a deck of playing cards. Every season, we are issued a set of cards, each set containing two different types of cards—costs and benefits. For instance, we might start a new job that has a great salary package and opportunities for career advance-ment. But this same job also requires that we work 80-hour weeks, infringing on our work/life balance boundaries.

In any particular season though, what we usually focus on are the costs. We'll spend our time trying to get rid of those cards, doing whatever we can to get them out of our hands. Our excitement about our job quickly turns to complaining, as we are constantly criticizing our boss and all the "extra" stuff our job requires of us. What we used to talk about as a bless-ing has now become a burden. So, eventually, we decide that the best way to get rid of our "cost" cards is to change seasons. We submit our résumé to a bunch of new organizations and eventually land ourselves a new job. When we do, "life" issues us a whole new set of cards, giving us a fresh set of costs and benefits.

The thing is, we don't approach our new season think-ing we'll get a new set of costs. We just think we get to keep our old benefits while gaining new ones, all while getting rid of the costs that were too high for us. But in the new season we don't always get to keep benefits from the old one and we *always* get a set of new costs. So, in our last job we were able to work from home and take personal time off (PTO) whenever we needed it. Even though our work was demanding, our boss rarely questioned anything we did. Now, we work for a boss who micromanages everything we do. PTO is harder to get approved than a law in Washington, D.C. The flexibility and independence we had is gone. But we didn't know this would be the case until *after* we changed jobs. If we knew these would be the new costs, we might not have decided to switch jobs in the first place!

The point of the illustration is that every season has costs, or more so, longings. When my sister was giving me her short but profound advice about marriage, this was what she was trying to tell me. She had come to realize that the season of marriage was no less difficult; the difficulty just took a different shape than it had in the last season. Furthermore, the joy she experienced in marriage was no greater than the joy she experienced as a single; it too just took a different shape. Neither season came without cost or benefit; they each just had their own unique mix.

Learning from Joshua

After Joshua's conversation with God, he goes on to lead Israel through the fulfillment of the promise God made to them through Abraham (Gen. 12:1–3). He leads two million people across the Jordan River into the Land of Canaan. I would encourage you to read through the rest of his story, for it is an exciting story of victory, with a bit of humbling defeat. But what always stands out to me from Joshua's story are some of the final words he gives to Israel at the very end of his life. He says,

> "Now therefore fear the LORD and serve him in sincerity and in faithfulness. Put away the gods that your fathers served beyond the River and in Egypt, and serve the LORD. And if it is evil in your eyes to serve the LORD, choose this day whom you will serve, whether the gods your fathers served in the region beyond the River, or the gods of the Amorites in whose land you dwell. But as for me and my house, we will serve the LORD." (Josh. 24:14–15)

In this final address to the people, Joshua reminds them of the opportunities they will have in the future to turn away from God. The world around them would give them ample opportunity to forsake the truth of God's character and promises for lies. They would be presented with the lie that these false gods were better than the one true God. In their moments of weakness or difficulty, they might be tempted to view these lies as truth. But by communicating his strong commitment to God, Joshua is telling the people, "No matter what happens, I will always believe that life with the Lord is better."

Longing Is Universal

While we don't like to think about it, the truth is that everyone experiences longing. We all have desires, or a set of expectations, that go unmet. The obvious one people tend to think of is singleness because what a single person lacks is very apparent. But longing doesn't just affect the singles out there. In my years of ministry, I think about all the people I've met who are struggling to navigate the brokenness in this world and the gap between the life they want and the life they have. Whether it's infertility, an absent parent, a terrible job, or unbearable in-laws, there is always a part of our life that is hard. Until Jesus returns, the brokenness of the world guarantees that each of us will walk with our own "limp."

Hopefully, by now you've realized that my goal is to help you walk in joy with your limp, giving you tools to bring with you into any season of life. Because, for many of you, your season of longing will end and you will be launched into a new one. In the beginning everything will be great, but as time wears on, you'll realize the new, hidden costs that were dealt to you. In that moment, my hope is that you would practice self-examination, lament, hope, remembrance, faith, and joy.

While I've talked about these six overarching habits as if they are a straight line, please know that many times they are not. You will find yourself rotating in and out of lament, while you are walking in faith and fighting to walk in joy at the same time. But, even if this process proves to be messy—and it probably will because that's how life usually goes—it will ground your soul in truth that is strong enough to handle the hard questions yet soft enough to handle your tears.

And, as you cycle through those six spiritual practices, what you will realize is that they all combine to form one overarching habit—*contentment*. Please know I intentionally have not mentioned this word up until this point. There are certain words in our Christian culture that while deeply significant, aren't too appreciated. Contentment is one of them. In my experience, people usually find it to be a bit lifeless and insensitive to the pain we feel. It can seem to communicate a life of quiet reservation rather than one of vibrant joy.

But the right word for the goal we are moving toward is contentment. Echoing the words of the apostle Paul in Philippians 4:11, spiritual maturity for us as believers includes the ability to remain steady in any season. This does not minimize our emotions or invalidate our pain, but rather it highlights the steadiness of Jeremiah 17:7, where we have roots that run wide in the truth of Scripture. Regardless of whether it is overly hot or cold, we live vibrant lives that bear fruit because we are rooted in a story that is greater than our pain. No matter what, we fight to find joy in the Lord, because we know, like Joshua, that life with him is better than anything the world provides us.

A New Vision for Life

I am a creature of habit. I have no problem eating the same meals every week, I tend to shop at the same stores, and I wear the same small rotation of clothes. I'm not opposed to change, but I also tend not to try to fix something that works. Especially when it took me a long time to get it right the first time!

One more habit I have has to do with my glasses. I buy a new pair of glasses every year. But I buy the same glasses every year. I probably have about three or four of the exact same style of glasses in my catch-all storage containers. But again, if it ain't broke, I ain't gonna fix it!

Throughout the year, my glasses inevitably get scratched up. But I never realize how bad they are until I put on my new pair of glasses. It never fails—once I put them on, I'm amazed at how long I went around with impaired vision. So why don't I notice the problem? Because the scratches don't show up on my glasses all at once. They show up gradually. Every time I drop them on the ground, use my shirt to wipe them, or leave them next to me in the bed while I sleep, a few scratches appear. With each iteration of bad-glasses behavior, the amount of scratches grows—yet never fast enough that I actually notice. Like I said before, it's not until I put on a new pair that I realize how bad the old ones were.

Slowly, over time, mishandled longing impairs our vision. With each iteration of disappointment that gets poorly processed (or not processed at all), things get more and more cloudy until it becomes hard to see. The thing is, though, we don't realize we can't see until we put on a new pair of "glasses." But once we do, our imagination for life gets restored.

When longing has made our vision for life fuzzy, the "new glasses" we need to put on is the story of the Bible. It gives us a place to bring our pain, but also helps us put it in perspective.

It reminds us that we are part of a larger story, where the possibilities for our life are bigger than the gap of longing we feel. These new glasses give us a renewed vision for our lives, encouraging us that not only can and will we be okay, but that we can and will thrive.

If we were in a room together having this conversation, I would probably leave you with one question: What would your life look like if you chose to wear the "new glasses" instead of your scratched-up ones?

Friend, we only get one life. Even if you want to exchange yours for another one, you can't and there are no do-overs. God gives us one shot to do with it what we wish. Pain and all.

Of all the options that will be made available to you, I hope you choose to *Embrace Your Life*.

Because even if our situation never changes, the God we serve is still good, and the life he has given us is still worth living because it's a beautiful life that we get to live with him.

Notes

Introduction: Embrace the Journey

1. Obviously, this sister's real name is not Charlene. I've changed her name and a few other details about the story to protect her identity. The same is true for every other person named in this book.

Chapter 1: Embrace Help

1. I don't own a TV, so I watch my shows when I hang out at my friends' or family's house.
2. https://www.thegospelcoalition.org/themelios/article/were-old-covenant-believers-indwelt-by-the-holy-spirit/
3. A. W. Tozer, *My Daily Pursuit: Devotions for Every Day* (Ventura, CA: Regal Books, 2013), 106.
4. Many scholars attribute authorship of Psalm 119 to David, though some think this could be Ezra or Daniel.

Chapter 2: (Don't) Embrace Avoidance

1. Timothy Keller, *Counterfeit Gods* (New York: Penguin Books, 2009), Kindle Edition.
2. Keller, *Counterfeit Gods*.

3. Rich Villodas, *The Deeply Formed Life: Five Transformative Values to Root Us in the Way of Jesus* (Colorado Springs: WaterBrook, 2020), 155.

4. J. Alasdair Groves and Winston T. Smith, *Untangling Emotions* (Wheaton: Crossway, 2019), 90–91.

Chapter 3: Embrace the Loss

1. https://www.shomreineshama.com/stages-of-mourning

2. Aubrey Sampson, *The Louder Song: Listening for Hope in the Midst of Lament* (Colorado Springs: NavPress, 2019), 12.

3. Mark Vroegop, "Dare to Hope in God," *Desiring God*, April 6, 2019, https://www.desiringgod.org/articles/dare-to-hope-in-god.

4. Todd J. Billings, *Rejoicing in Lament* (Grand Rapids: Brazos Press, 2015), 58.

5. Jemar Tisby, *The Color of Compromise: The Truth about the American Church's Complicity in Racism* (Grand Rapids: Zondervan, 2019), 202–203.

6. Lyrics to the traditional Negro spiritual "Didn't My Lord Deliver Daniel?" (public domain).

Chapter 4: Embrace Hope

1. Kathleen H. O'Connor, *Lamentations and the Tears of the World* (Maryknoll, NY: Orbis Books), 57.

2. Paul Tripp, *Suffering: Gospel Hope When Life Doesn't Make Sense* (Wheaton: Crossway, 2018), 136.

3. Tripp, *Suffering*, 136.

4. Ed Love, *The Coming God: Pursuing a Theology of Hope* (2011), *Doctor of Ministry*, Paper 5, http://digitalcommons.georgefox.edu/dmin/5.

Chapter 5: Embrace Who God Is

1. https://www.merriam-webster.com/dictionary/character

2. Authors like Jen Wilkin, Arthur W. Pink, J. I. Packer, and R. C. Sproul have done a great job writing about the character of God. I would encourage you to check out their books for an extensive discussion on the topic.

3. Michael D. Williams, *Far as the Curse Is Found* (Phillipsburg, NJ: P&R Publishing, 2005), 41.

4. Jen Wilkin, *None Like Him: 10 Ways God Is Different from Us (and Why That's a Good Thing)* (Wheaton: Crossway, 2016), 71.

5. Wilkin, *None Like Him*, 74.

6. Arthur W. Pink, *The Attributes of God* (Grand Rapids: Baker Books, 1975), 40.

7. Wilkin, *None Like Him*, 44.

8. Paul Tripp, *Suffering* (Wheaton: Crossway, 2018), 136.

9. Pink, *The Attributes of God*, 66.

10. https://www.gotquestions.org/Bible-faithfulness.html

11. Williams, *Far as the Curse Is Found*, 115.

12. Tripp, *Suffering*, 148.

13. Tripp, *Suffering*, 156.

14. I've said it before, but I'll repeat it again: authors like Jen Wilkin, Arthur W. Pink, J. I. Packer, and R. C. Sproul have done a great job writing about the character of God. I would encourage you to check out their books for an extensive discussion on the topic. I would also encourage you to make a list of the attributes of God and leave it in your Bible or journal for quick reference.

Chapter 6: Embrace Who You Are

1. https://mfa.gov.il/MFA/IsraelExperience/AboutIsrael/Spotlight/Pages/Jewish%20Sacred%20Texts.aspx

Chapter 7: Embrace Faith

1. Tom Constable, *Tom Constable's Expository Notes on the Bible* (Galaxie Software, 2003), Joshua 3:14.

2. Dr. Tony Evans, *CSB Tony Evans Study Bible* (Nashville: Holman, 2019), 14.

3. "Remembering 1963: Fannie Lou Hamer Arrested and Beaten in Winona Mississippi," *Equal Justice Initiative*, June 6, 2018, https://eji.org/news/remembering-1963-fannie-lou-hamer-arrested-and-beaten-winona-mississippi.

4. K. J. Ramsey, *This Too Shall Last: Finding Grace When Suffering Lingers* (Grand Rapids: Zondervan, 2020), 59.

Chapter 8: Embrace Joy

1. Scott Swain, "The Heart Is Not a Cup (There's a Better Metaphor)," *The Gospel Coalition*, May 8, 2020, https://www.thegospelcoalition.org/article/heart-not-cup/.

2. Swain, "The Heart Is Not a Cup."

3. "Brené Brown on Joy and Gratitude," *Global Leadership Network*, November 21, 2018, https://globalleadership.org/articles/leading-yourself/brene-brown-on-joy-and-gratitude/.

4. Dr. Brené Brown, *Daring Greatly* (New York: Penguin Random House, 2012), 123.

5. Adele Ahlberg Calhoun, *Spiritual Disciplines Handbook* (Downers Grove, IL: InterVarsity Press, 2005), 29.

6. Calhoun, *Spiritual Disciplines Handbook*, 29.

7. Calhoun, *Spiritual Disciplines Handbook*, 27.